D1611968

# The Imagery of Sophocles'
## *Antigone*

# The Imagery of
# Sophocles' *Antigone*

## A STUDY
## OF POETIC LANGUAGE
## AND STRUCTURE

By Robert F. Goheen

PRINCETON, NEW JERSEY
PRINCETON UNIVERSITY PRESS

1951

MANUFACTURED IN THE UNITED STATES OF AMERICA BY
PRINCETON UNIVERSITY PRESS AT PRINCETON, NEW JERSEY

*TO*

*M. S. G.*

# CONTENTS

CONTENTS

# The Imagery of Sophocles'
## *Antigone*

"I conceive then a word, as poetry is concerned with it, . . . to be a component of an act of the mind so subtly dependent on other components of this act and of other acts that it can be distinguished from these interactions only as a convenience of discourse. It sounds nonsense to say that a word is its interactions with other words; but that is a short way of saying the thing which Poetics is most in danger always of overlooking. Words only work together. We understand no word except in and through its interactions with other words" (I. A. Richards, "The Interactions of Words" in *The Language of Poetry*, Princeton, 1942, p. 74).

"The structure meant is a structure of meanings, evaluations and interpretations; and the principle of unity which informs it seems to be one of balancing and harmonizing connotations, attitudes and meanings. But even here one needs to make important qualifications: the principle is not one which involves the arrangement of various elements into homogeneous groupings, pairing like with like. It unites the like with the unlike. It does not unite them, however, by the simple process of allowing one connotation to cancel out another nor does it reduce the contradictory attitudes to harmony by a process of subtraction. The unity is not a unity of the sort to be achieved by the reduction and simplification appropriate to an algebraic formula. It is a positive unity, not a negative; it represents not a residue but an achieved harmony" (Cleanth Brooks, *The Well Wrought Urn*, New York, Harcourt, Brace and Company, 1947, pp. 178-9).

# CHAPTER I · INTRODUCTION

## *Program*

THIS essay centers upon one element of the *Antigone*, the poetic imagery, in the belief that such a study can illumine the role of Sophocles' poetry in his drama and add precision and fullness to our understanding of the meanings of his works. The images are only one of the poet's means of communication. But as such they are important, and they provide a rewarding means of entry into the complex structure of interworking parts which such a play forms. The images not only give brilliance or emotional color to individual expressions; they also point up the progress of the action and develop meanings essential to the whole.

The major undertaking here is to illustrate the workings of dominant images or master tropes in the *Antigone*. Six groups of recurrent images, forming patterns or sequences, serve to arouse and establish connections of thought, emotion, and judgment from part to part of the play. They afford developing insights into the nature of the characters and at the same time evoke larger issues within which the significance of the characters' actions is to be viewed. Not only does the recurrence of these images give them heightened prominence in the play; their extending relationships also permit more direct analysis of their functional or structural contributions to the work as a whole than is possible with many of the play's other images. There is a further external reason for centering upon the dominant images in this way. Because our knowledge of the nuances of classical Greek is limited, there must always be some uncertainty as to the full connotations of any image in a work of Greek poetry. This barrier is less serious in connection with a number of more or less consistent, mutually supporting images than it is for the more self-contained expressions.

The final two chapters draw upon the evidence of the dominant images to interpret the odes and the divergent modes of expression of the two chief characters. The next to last chapter considers in detail the sensuous and imagistic aspects of three of the odes in an effort to make clearer their complex meanings in the larger poem of which they are parts. The concluding chapter illustrates additional ways in which imagery and expression are developed to depict the major characters and to express their divergent attitudes and their disparate methods of judgment. Here we have also close illustration for the interrelationship of the imagery and the theme of the tragedy, and an analysis of the theme and content of the tragedy is reserved to this point when it can be offered in the light of all the evidence at our disposal.

Primarily we are seeking to sharpen and enrich our understanding of a play which has been enjoyed through the ages and about which much excellent criticism has already been written. No radically new interpretation of the theme of the play is to be offered. But the study of imagery can make a positive contribution to our understanding of the play's basic ideas, its inner consistency. The "idea" of the *Antigone* has been the subject of as much conflicting opinion as that of any play.[1] Our study can support certain lines of this criticism with assurance and can help to reject others no less decisively. It is in great measure through the patterns of imagery which the poet has created to convey and support his theme that we can know what that theme is, and it is through these patterns that we are led to share in the subtler insights and to feel some of the deepest human implications which the poet has built into and upon his theme.

Preliminary to fuller consideration in subsequent chapters, we may set forth here briefly the nexus of ideas and attitudes which lies at the heart of the play's structure. Essentially the *Antigone* is, as C. M. Bowra has recently described it, "a tragedy of human folly [wherein] the illusions of men resist and rebut the claims of a higher reality and truth."[2] Blindness of soul causes a man in high position to oppose the final moral order of things, represented in particular by the traditional sanctity of burial and by a woman of unusual emotional insight and determination. For such error men are

4

finally responsible to the gods, and they are made to suffer punishment for the destructive acts of pride and irreverence to which such blindness leads them. The theme of course is not the play. The detail which gives these general ideas concrete and intense meaning in the play is essential for more than just a vague understanding of them. As we examine important features of this detail and see their effectiveness in developing and determining the meaning of the whole, we should come to see that Sophocles in this play is an artist who works his medium so as to express much of the complexity and many of the cross-tensions of human experience. A full experiencing of the *Antigone* offers no banal or simple solution: it brings awareness of increasingly fine distinctions and of complex perceptions brought complexly into unity.

## A Word on Method

Our attention will be directed primarily to elements of the imagery whose structural and thematic functions are readily observable. We are not concerned with general qualities of style or abstract critical principles except as they apply in the particular and there show their force and are there illustrated or verified. Other elements of Sophocles' diction do, of course, have bearing for the full understanding of the play, as in helping to create tone, mark attitude, and project quality of mind. One's critical principles do, inevitably, influence one's criticism. But though this study will be seen to offer some concrete support for certain "modern" critical ideas, this is, I feel, a secondary product and one whose proof lies in the concrete analyses offered. Therefore I have not included here a lengthy description either of modern criticism or of the over-all qualities of Sophocles' style. Those who are even generally familiar with both will not require further explanations of the methods used. Anyone who desires a fuller introduction either to the general characteristics of Sophoclean diction or to the specific critical principles applied to it here will find them briefly set forth in the Postscript.

Briefly, three aspects of poetry, brought into special attention by the recent trend of criticism, underlie this study.

They are : the richness or multivalence of poetic language, the interanimation of the parts and the sources of tension within poems, and the fact that "in the best poetry metaphor is not merely a prettification but rather a primary element in the structure, a basic constituent in form."[3] These facts of poetic language and structure have not been totally unrecognized or unexplored in the field of Greek poetry. Writing sometime about A.D. 100, "Longinus" was touching on these principles, or at least the second of them, when he praised Sappho's poem for its exact and intense unification of conflicting images and also in the sections where he treats "composition" or verbal structure.[4] And in the last few years W. B. Stanford's excellent studies have done much to clarify the role of metaphor, the presence of intensifying ambiguities, and the use of recurrent imagery in Greek poetry.[5] Another eminent name may be added from the classical field. Writing in 1942 Eduard Fränkel exhorted students of Greek tragedy to a method of approach which would center upon critical words or word clusters and exploit contextual interrelationships of meaning. He wrote, "We may begin with observing words, their meaning, their structure, and their order, and end with observing characteristic habits of the poet's mind in shaping dramatic characters, bringing about a tragic tension, and revealing his religious convictions."[6] So although this method is relatively new and is not yet completely developed for Greek poetry (which presents the special problems of a "dead" language), precedent is good and the objective eminently worth attaining.

In any case, and certainly in any extended view of western literature, only momentary surprise should be occasioned by the applicability for so ancient a work as the *Antigone* of methods of criticism whose development as effective methods of poetic analysis has largely occurred within the twentieth century. The "modernity" of classical antiquity has often been demonstrated. In literature particularly, the Greco-Roman has been such a strong and many-sided influence upon the English tradition that there is little cause to wonder at the recognition, however late, of procedures common to the best poetry of the two cultures.

## Dimensions of the Tragic Form

Our aim, then, is to center upon key words and word patterns of the play so that we may see more precisely and fully what the *Antigone* is and is about. This is not to seek, or permit, a sharp distinction between the poetry and the drama of that work. The structure is both poetic and dramatic; the two aspects are inseparable and mutually complementary. Language expresses character, helps to create action, and brings into the whole elements of meaning extending beyond the particular situation of the plot. The plot and characters in turn not only condition the use of language but are vehicles for its symbolic values. In a sense, the plot of agents in action is the basic image. All the other images and image patterns are related to it and function with it to form the total meaning. To apprehend the total meaning we must therefore see the various developments of the verbal imagery in their functional bearings upon the large image which is the dramatic plot formed "according to the rules of probability and necessity."

In its original form, Attic tragedy is one of the most complex forms of art known. Music, song, and the dance were integral elements of the medium. Even with these elements almost totally lost to us, as they are, the Greek tragedies we possess offer a highly organized richness in their means of communication. Unlike the modern opera to which it is often compared, Greek tragedy did not subordinate plot and character—or, if you will, drama—to music and the dance. This is clear from the extant tragedies. In general, the plot or conflict of agents in action is, as Aristotle observed, the central structural feature. And in every extant Greek tragedy the language, or element of diction, is a highly and skillfully developed element. To some extent perhaps this is a happy accident. A large open-air theater, heavy costuming, and masks imposed limitations on physical action and facial expression which by modern standards must seem severe. But all these factors also meant that the words of the speakers had to bear a heavy share of the load. Thus we find in Greek tragedy, as in Elizabethan poetic drama, a thorough exploitation of the subtle and positive resources of poetic language. "Imagery of all kinds, ambivalences of meaning and suggestion, words made uniquely potent and momentous by the circumstances of context, figures of speech, in particular metaphors"—all these are used by the three Attic tragedians to create and to enrich their desired effects.[7]

The total structure of the tragedy has therefore two significant dimensions: a horizontal (time) dimension and a vertical (meaning, value) dimension. The horizontal dimension is the progressing movement of the tragedy, especially of the story or plot, from a beginning to a middle to an end. The vertical dimension is what the tragedy as a whole means. This, too, starts with the plot—the sequence of actions as symbolizing something or representing certain universals—but it includes also the choral and poetic components, which contribute to the total content kinds of perception and modes of meaning that are to some extent over and above the specific actions of the characters.

Aristotle's definition of Greek tragedy in the *Poetics* expresses concisely the basic horizontal structure of our play, its nature as drama. "Tragedy," he says, "is an imitation of an action that is serious, having magnitude and complete in itself . . . in the form of action, not of narrative, with incidents arousing pity and fear, wherewith to accomplish a catharsis [purgation] of such emotions."[8] By implication in its term *imitation* the Aristotelian definition recognizes that the action of a tragedy is symbolic of universal human traits and problems.[9] By general implication from the rest of the *Poetics*, Aristotle is, I believe, rightly demanding that all the components of a tragedy must be closely related to the prime dramatic factor of plot or action—the action of characters developed with intensity and consistency according to the laws of probability and necessity. But other than this, the Aristotelian analysis, as we have it, does not include much of what I have termed the vertical structure of Greek tragedy.

8

For example, it recognizes but hastens past the fact that a tragedy may have a fuller significance than its ability to arouse and drain out our raw emotions. Except for one pregnant remark on metaphor, which is not developed,[10] Aristotle relegates diction to a monosemantic ornamental role. And Aristotle does not consider how the various elements of the form, besides the plot, are organized into the rich complexes of meaning to be found in such plays as the *Oresteia*, the Oedipus tragedies, and the *Medea*, to cite a few of many examples.

From our point of view, both the range (vertical) and the compelling artistic unity (both vertical and horizontal) of a tragedy like the *Antigone* depend upon the skill with which the various poetic and lyric means of communication are employed to complement, illumine, and extend the meanings of the dramatic actions. Much of the essence of Greek tragedy is the way in which it sets human problems in some kind of final perspective, involving more than the surface of life. Much of its quality and its power lies in the multiple means employed to explore, develop, and focus such problems in depth.

## The Fact of Recurrence

Recurrence of imagery is a fact of the *Antigone* which we have already stated to be one of the keys to the total structure, and it is a fact with which we shall be concerned for most of the rest of this essay. It is of significance for us in several ways and on several levels.

At a rather elementary level it serves as an indication that an unobtrusive image or one which might otherwise be regarded as "dead" is in fact alive within a pattern of meanings created by the poet about it. Consider, for example, the military terms in the opening speech of the play:

And now what is this new thing which they say that the general (*stratêgon*) has just had heralded to the city and all its people: Do you know? Have you heard? Or do you fail to see that the evils of your enemies are marching (*steichonta*) on your friends? (7-10)[11]

When Antigone refers to Creon here as the *stratêgos* (a general term for the leader of the state in many tragedies, a military general, a chief executive in the Athenian state) the term may seem only general and of not much particular significance at first. At the same time, the implication of military rigor to be felt in the term is given support by the military implication of the other word, *steichonta*, which follows closely behind. This later term often means only to proceed, but it is connected closely with marching and military columns. Together these two images in the overtones of Antigone's first reference to Creon have connection to, and show their vitality in their bearing upon, Creon's second and crucial statement of political principle (639-80), which, as we shall see more fully, rests upon a military conception and includes obedience "to small orders and just orders and orders of the opposite kind" (667). And here, as Antigone's initial, latent characterization of Creon's manner of rule foresees, well in advance of the vision of the other characters, the limited character of that rule and expresses it in just the terms which Creon later brings into the open, the recurrences of military imagery take us to a further level of meaning and a more internal kind of awareness—that of Antigone's intuitive knowledge and its validity, despite the general discredit which it suffers for over half of the play.

Another example is worth noticing, for it involves an almost hoary metaphor being called to life and being so developed as to take us into the clash of points of view on one of the central issues of the play. This is the sequence built on *hyperbainein* (to overstep, transgress) in application to law and religious principles.[12] The first appearance is 449. Creon asks Antigone,

> Did you then dare to overstep these laws?

She replies affirmatively and in her famous speech of defense presents the righteousness of her conduct as against his view that he, a mortal, could override (*hyperdramein*) the unwritten and imperishable laws of the gods (454-5).[13] Creon returns to his original expression in 481, and the momentary balance and clash of these images subsides for the time being. But following this scene, the Chorus recalls Creon's original term to generalize upon Zeus's invincible power and law of retribution against human *transgression* (604-14). As a result of the previous exchange with this image in relation to human and divine law, suggestive overtones are aroused when the Chorus continues and applies this general theme with a further pedal image:

> For far-ranging expectation is to many men a comfort but to many the deceit which follows light desire. Disillusionment comes to him who knows not until he burn his foot in the hot fire. (615-19)[14]

Then in the next scene, the Haimon scene, Creon returns again, with condemnation, to *transgressors* of the law (663), and near the end of the scene a related image is used against him by his son:

> CR. Shameless one, bringing charges against your father.
> HA. No! for I see you miss what is just.
> CR. Am I wrong when I respect the rights that are mine?
> HA. This is not respect, to trample (*patôn*) the honors and offices of the gods. (742-5)

(However slightly Creon seems convinced here by his son's clear echo of Antigone's argument, from this point on he stops talking about "law" and stands instead more openly for power.) Only once, after the catastrophe has come down on his head, does he again mention law and then it is in full humility (1113-14). And in the very end it is Creon who has both *trampled* on his own chances of happiness and who, for his late recognition of his error, has been *trampled* by the final moral forces of the play. So Creon himself puts the matter in the last scene of the play:

> Now surely some god struck down on my head, constraining me with a great weight. He drove me into wild ways, overturning my joy so that it is trampled down (*lakpatêton*). O my woe! (1272-5)[15]

This is, moreover, only one of several instances where an image which Creon starts against the opposition rises gradually to more explicit, concrete form and turns against him to create a poignant irony in respect to his judgment. Thus the recurrent images of this sequence not only help to develop the large questions of the nature and source of law which are raised within the play; they interwork with the treatments of evaluation, vision, goal, and governance (personal, public, and final) which are offered by the dominant image sequences.

In general, the recurrent images of the play have at least a double value. They have the denotative value of their particular use, in a limited context. But they also take meanings from the pattern of similar images of which they are a part. And each pattern is to some extent qualified by the others. Their values are such as to characterize the points of view of different figures in the play and set them in sharp opposition on fundamental matters. At the same time the sequences of recurrent images, in a still further symbolic role, help to bring into the play the basic issues or facts of human experience which the dramatist saw as relevant to the understanding of his tragic theme.

The six dominant image sequences which accomplish this most fully for the *Antigone* are those which recur with the greatest degree of frequency—excepting the many images which can be grouped under the general heading of images of bodily action. Images from four fields of experience recur with particularly marked frequency. They are money and merchandising, warfare and military activity, animals and the control of animals, and the sea and sailing. Besides these, images of disease and images of marriage form significant sequences slightly more restricted in diversity and frequency of application. Generally speaking, the monetary, military, and animal patterns have characterization as a prominent function, especially with respect to Creon. They develop, that is, telling characteristics and colors in his mode of judgment and bring out acutely the implications of shortsightedness in the methods of governance to which these characteristics lead him. The nautical, disease, and marital patterns have as their most obvious function the integration to the play of more ultimate facts and mysteries about the nature of evil and the relation of man and the gods. But the two sides of the matter are closely connected, and each sequence of images shares in some measure both of these general functions. This perhaps will become most apparent in the sequence of animal imagery. Used chiefly by Creon or in relation to him, this imagery both characterizes him as a person and serves a critical role for the understanding of the man-god relationship and its decisive moral bearing within the tragedy.

# CHAPTER II · IMAGERY OF
# EVALUATION AND CONTROL

## The Money Sequence

CLOSE to the heart of the dramatic conflict of the *Antigone* are radical differences in the kinds and sources of human motivation embodied in the major figures, and among the questions which the tragedy asks us are those of the value and the valuation of different sorts of basic motivation. A well-developed pattern of monetary and mercantile metaphors help to delineate these divergences and these questions.

The character who most consistently and emphatically employs such images to judge human conduct is Creon. In various situations, especially when his anger is aroused against opposition which he does not entirely understand, he calls upon monetary images and seeks to brand as money-mad the agents who oppose him. The strongest and fullest expression of this attitude is in the Teiresias scene immediately preceding the dramatic peripety. Faced with Teiresias' warning that the city is polluted because of his course of action and advised by the blind seer to take counsel from one who counsels to his *profit* (1032),[1] Creon counters:

> Old man, . . . many times have I been sold for export
> and made into cargo by the tribe of seers. Make your
> profits. Buy and sell electrum from Sardis if you wish,
> and Indian gold. But you shall not cover that man
> [Polyneices] with a tomb. (1033-9)

The image, touched off in this instance by Teiresias' quiet "if the counsellor speak to your profit," continues. Creon ends the speech with the threat:

> They fall, ancient Teiresias, with a shameful fall, even
> ever clever men—when they speak shameful counsel in
> noble guise for the sake of gain. (1045-7)

He matches Teiresias' further warnings with further expressions of the same order:

The whole class of seers has always been fond of silver. (1055)
Out with your secret. But don't speak for profit. (1061)
Be sure of this. You will not speculate (*empoleson*) with my resolve. (1063)

Finally Teiresias cannot restrain his anger and, using a variant of Creon's monetary imagery (1077), he voices the prophetic warning which subdues once and for all Creon's opposition and forms the turning point of the action.

Prior to the Teiresias scene there are several strong monetary images, as well as several less vivid occurrences, which together lend force and carry implications to its sustained appearances in that scene. For example, Creon's first pronouncement of his edict, including the death penalty for its violators, ends on this note:

CH. There is no one so much a fool as to be enamoured of death.
CR. Indeed just this will be his wage (*misthos*). Yet, time and again money with its hopes leads men to ruin. (220-2)

Again in the same scene, when Creon learns that his edict has already been broken, his analysis of the situation takes the form of an exuberant personification of money as the root and teacher of all evil:

Nothing so evil as silver ever grew to be current (*nomisma*) among men. This sacks cities; this drives men from their homes; this teaches and warps honest minds to approach deeds of shame. It has shown men all sorts of villainy and the knowledge of every kind of impiety. But whoever did this deed for a fee have accomplished just this: sooner or later they will pay the penalty. (295-303)[2]

Before the close of this scene, the charge that the Guards

have sold out for silver or other material profit is made three more times by Creon (310-12, 322, 325-6).

Just as Creon's suspicion and his monetary estimate of the character of the opposition here is soon proved wrong, so, in the Teiresias scene the reviving of the monetary images and of the bribery theme serves to signal the limitation of Creon's perception and prepares for the dramatic recognition. This implication is supported by the use of monetary terms as they are assigned to other speakers in the first half of the play. Haimon, for instance, suggests to Creon that much more is involved than his eye sees and suggests that Antigone is in fact worthy of "golden honor" (699). He urges, too, that, so far as human goods or property are concerned, intelligence is by far the supreme endowment from the gods to men (683-4). Thus in both these instances Haimon uses expressions from a sphere which Creon has brought to the foreground. But Haimon uses them in order to argue the value of certain elements of human nature and conduct which he feels that his father has underestimated.

Antigone's employment of monetary images does the same sort of thing more fully. The first appearance is in her initial explicit reference to Polyneices. She tells Ismene of Creon's edict—how no one is to bury Polyneices or even mourn him but all are ordered:

> To leave him unwept, unburied, a sweet treasure (*glykyn thêsauron*) for carrion birds to look upon and feast upon at will. (29-30)[3]

Even as Antigone calls her brother's corpse a "sweet treasure" (a lucky find and rich fare) for carrion birds, it is clear that this treasure is also the repository of her dearest affections, is her own "sweet treasure" which she means to try to protect. In the same way later, when Antigone has been caught and is confronted with the threat of death, she can speak of the "profit" of death, since she has done that to which family allegiance and her sense of right directed her:

> If I am to die before my time, I reckon this too a gain (*kerdos*). For when one lives among evils as I do, how

can he die and not make gain (*kerdos pherei*)? . . . But
if I had let my mother's son die and lie unburied, for
that I should have grieved. (461-8)[4]

In paraphrase, the breaker of the edict has indeed worked
for "gain," even for what is to her a real "treasure." But
this is "gain" of a sort and a desire for "profit" in a sense
which Creon has not considered in the first episode and whose
value he does not realize until after Teiresias' final warning. When the catastrophe has brought that realization emphatically home to Creon, there recur near the end of the play
two dramatically ironic echoes of the monetary imagery which
turn back on his earlier mode of judging, or misjudging,
human conduct. One appears in the mouth of the first Messenger (1168-71); the other is expressed by the Chorus.
(1326)[5]

In the major developments of this pattern of monetary
images, questions of insight, we see, are raised alongside
questions of motivation and evaluation. As Antigone, and
to a lesser degree Haimon and Teiresias, share these same
terms which are characteristic of Creon's judgment of human
nature but apply them to denote motives and standards quite
different from the venality which he is so prone to ascribe to
others, the underlying clash within the surface parallelism
helps to make both intense and deep-reaching the separation
between their points of view. The words are the same but the
very similarity makes for further misunderstanding instead
of for understanding, because the views of human nature
and its significant sources of action, which the terms embody,
are different. In some measure this is a procedure and an
implication common to all of the image sequences and to other
concepts in the play—the recurrent split of the two protagonists over certain common words.[6] In this pattern, as elsewhere, it dramatizes the difficulty of knowing motives and
judging actions; for even as the characters use the same terms
to each other we see them blind to each other's meaning.

This close relation of the question of valuation with the
question of sight (insight) is particularized for us by two

17

further monetary images. They are both images of false coinage, which at critical, matching points in the action demand that one must look below the surface of things to test their genuine value. In his opening speech on his right to govern and his principles of government, Creon offers us the first of these images in these words:

> It is impossible to discover any man's nature, thought or judgment before he is shown *tested and rubbed down* (*entribês*) by public duties and the laws. (175-7)

The expression involves an old maxim, attributed to Bias and others of the Seven Sages, that "Authority shows the man." But there is almost certainly a reference to the detection of spurious coinage by wear, the wear of repeated use and possibly the rubbing of a touchstone.[7] The numerous other monetary terms in the play should make us recognize these connotations, but in case they do not, we have the image given to us again in a more striking form.

It recurs in Teiresias' final warning to Creon and is in part a specific and ironic answer to Creon's charges of venality. After having been goaded by Creon into voicing his most secret and dire forebodings, Teiresias foretells that Creon will pay with one of his own offspring for having wronged Antigone and mistreated Polyneices' corpse. The nether gods also have been wronged and their avengers lie in wait for Creon. And then Teiresias says:

> And in respect to these things, see if I speak as one just gilded over (*katêrgyrômenos*); for the rub and test (*tribê*) of no great time will show the wails of men and women in your house. (1077-9)[8]

For Creon the testing factor (whether like the touchstone or the use of many hands) has been the laws and their administrations, and the course of the action from this point on shows very clearly that his "mind, thought, and judgment" in the proclamation and administration of his laws have been of inferior metal. For himself Teiresias claims the test of time and, by implication, of the will of the gods. These on the contrary in his case reveal that his words and the standards of conduct for which he speaks are indeed genuine. The two images appear at critical and matching positions within the play: Creon's initial statement of his principles and Teiresias' final speech which condemns and causes a reappraisal of those principles. And together these images of coinage help to show that Creon's manner of judgment is superficial, though specious, in its pragmatic rationality. Thus they help to create the realization that below the level of "realistic" politics lie deeper moral values and moral forces which must be taken into account in the business of government.

## The Military Sequence

The nature and quality of civil control espoused by the various forces in the tragedy and the problem of its relationships with individual insight and motive find partial expression in recurrent images drawn from military objects and procedures. Further, more basic aspects of the same issues are developed in the animal imagery to which we shall come next. The patterns are interworked so as to support and complement each other's implications. But within the tragedy the sequence of military images gives us, in its own right, a skillfully graded and subtly progressing insight into the kind of civic order that matches (or is likely to result from) the kind of valuation which Creon applies to personal motives.

The initial development of the pattern is quiet and suggestive. In the first three instances, which occur in the prologue, the concrete and emotional overtones of the expression are presented as latent indications which act indirectly to impress their implications on the later developments of the action. As we have observed, Antigone introduces military terminology in the very first speech of the play, when she queries her sister:

And now what is this new thing which they say the *general* has just *had heralded* to the city and all its people? Do you know? Have you heard? Or do you fail to see that the evils of your enemies are *marching* on your friends? (7-10)

19

The blending of concrete and general, of traditional terminology and a specific feeling of antipathy on Antigone's part in this expression have already been discussed. It is only necessary to note that the reference to Creon's decision as an edict announced by herald helps to develop the presentation of him as a military governor and so to add to Antigone's implication of his high-handedness. This is made apparent later in the scene, for when she is opposed by Ismene, Antigone turns the term against her sister:

> Oh speak out. You will be much the more hateful if you keep silent and do not *herald out* to everyone these plans of mine. (86-7)

By emotional implication as well as by direct statement Antigone thus dissociates herself and places her sister in Creon's ranks. Ismene, on the other hand, in the same scene meets exactly these implications and tries to counter them when she argues:

> But think on this, that we are women, not made to war (*machoumena*) against men. (61-2)

Whereas, that is, Antigone feels a military power and autocratic kind of authority raised against her and will contest it, even with her bare hands (43), Ismene is more cautious and urges their feminine weakness as reason to avoid this same contest.[9]

In the larger context these unobtrusive images and their interplay prepare for the understanding of Creon's attitude and the presentation of his principles of control when those are exhibited more fully. His first uses of military terminology are also unobtrusive, such ones as might easily mark a leader recently engaged in the defense of his city by arms. In his first speech, for example, he compliments the Chorus of elders with the suggestion that their counsel has been a strong wall of defense about the family of Laius:

> When he [Oedipus] perished, you still stood with firm-grounded counsel about their children. (168-9)

Later he bids the Chorus be *skopoi* (watchers, but usually military look-outs or spies) of his edict, and they, with perhaps significant insight, take his meaning first to be actual guards posted at the corpse (215-17). And soon after this, when the Guard enters but holds back his news behind a screen of anticipatory excuses, Creon catches him short with two images that are probably also of military origin:

> Your *aim* shows skill, and you manage to *fence* the matter *off* from yourself all round. Apparently you have news of a strange sort. (241-2)[10]

But the key locus in the sequence of military images, for which these others prepare, is the Haimon scene. In the first part of this scene Creon delivers a lengthy speech, designed not only to turn his son against Antigone but also to express his principles of domestic and civil order. A military basis for these precepts is sounded in Creon's opening sentence (in which, incidentally, Creon quite misses the equivocal nature of his son's preceding words):

> Yes, just this, my son, should be your heart's disposition, to hold your post (*opisthen hestanai*) behind your father's will in all matters. (639-40)[11]

In itself this introductory image of a soldier posted behind his leader foretells in some measure, as Jebb points out, the tone in which Creon presently enforces the value of discipline. But at the end of the speech the military suggestion is caught up and brought emphatically to the fore in two extended images:

> . . . whomever the city may establish, this one must be obeyed in small things and just things and things of the opposite sort. And this man,[12] I should venture, not only would rule well but would accept well being ruled. In a storm of spears he would stand where posted (*prostetagmenon*) a worthy and honorable comrade in ranks (*parastatên*).[13] But anarchy is surpassed by no other evil. This destroys cities; this makes households desolate. This in battle brings shattered rout of spear;

while obedience to orders, as the ranks hold straight,
saves the limbs and lives of most. (666-76)[14]

In all probability the eulogy of the values of order and discipline in these terms struck a familiar note of appeal for the
original audience, even though we can no longer assume that
the young Athenians in the theater recognized in Creon's
speech specific references to the Attic ephebic oath.[15] Some
sort of military training for the service of the state must have
been a normal experience for young men of Athens during
the mid-fifth century B.C., and the fact that the youthful
Haimon is here the recipient of Creon's lecture therefore adds
to the seeming appropriateness of Creon's use of military
examples.

But at the same time there are further significances to the
imagery and mode of expression in the speech whose effect is
to raise suspicion rather than approval for Creon's views.
The military images frame the statement of principles and
infuse it from both ends to suggest that the final basis, if
not the complete purport, of Creon's views here is military.
This element in the tone of the passage is by all counts antithetical to Athenian views of youthful training and the function of the state in the fifth century so far as we know them.[16]
And the suggestion of a totalitarian basis in the speech is
further developed by the almost "Freudian slip" whereby
Creon betrays a demand for absolute obedience, such as we
know only too well to be a characteristic of a military mode
of thought when carried beyond its proper provinces. This is
where Creon says,

> Whomever the city may establish, this man must be
> obeyed in small things and just things *and things of the
> opposite sort.* (666-7)

It is extremely difficult to imagine the original audience feeling in complete rapport with this sentiment. And there is no
evidence to indicate that they would, or that the poet expected
that they would, even though, to be sure, they expected military training for their youths and even though allegiance
to the state above their private interests was rightfully de-

manded of them in many aspects of their lives. But to qualify this statement of principles still further within the play there is a noteworthy responsion here to Creon's earlier personification of money (295-301). The half-personification of Anarchy in these lines clearly echoes expressions used in the earlier instances, so that one is invited again to question the depth of Creon's perceptions into human motivations.[17] The impinging of these two image sequences here seems, indeed, to suggest that Creon's views of law and order in military terms are part of a more far-reaching limitation and inadequacy of view.

In the later parts of the Haimon scene, lesser sustaining recurrences of the military sequence appear. Haimon in replying to his father endeavors at first to meet him on his own grounds so far as possible. It is, he says, his natural function as his father's son

> to scout out (*proskopein*) in your behalf all things that
> men say or do or find to blame. (688-9)[18]

Creon, however, reacts violently against the information and intelligence which Haimon goes on to report from his observation of the dark regions of popular feeling. They flare into open argument in which the conflict of autocratic and democratic ideas of government finally become explicit (732-9). And immediately following these lines, Creon again draws on a military metaphor to dismiss his son's democratical notions as special pleading for Antigone (740).

The next recurrence of military images is in the Teiresias scene; all the remaining military metaphors are, in fact, concentrated in this pivotal scene. Here Creon's half angry, half disdainful reaction to Teiresias' first warning begins with a simile from bowmen:

> Old man, like bowmen at a target, all of you bend your
> bows at me; not even by you seers have I been left
> untried. (1033-5)[19]

When Teiresias later is aroused to express his full insight, he uses a parallel simile to conclude his warning to Creon and to drive home the reality of his threats in Creon's own language:

> Since you provoke me, archer-like and in anger I have
> sped such [warnings] at you—shafts to pierce the heart
> and fasten there. Their hot sting you shall not escape.
> (1084-6)[20]

The obvious repetition gives direct point and edge to Teiresias'
reply, while also providing a link and balance within the
particular exchange of speeches. But at a deeper level, in
this episode the military images which have tended to mark
Creon's attitude and policies can also be felt to be reacting
against him at the turning point of dramatic action, much
as do the images of the monetary and animal patterns. For
closely following this exchange, two additional, less specialized military expressions appear, as though to reflect Creon's
former attitude and show its limitations. Both occur, significantly, in the crisis of Creon's "recognition" where he seeks
to alter his policy and forestall the catastrophe. The first is in
his initial comment on Teiresias' angry exit, an expression
of fear and self-doubt somewhat vaguely worded:

> I know too well [his proven truthfulness] and my mind
> is troubled. For to give ground (*eikathein*) is dire, but
> to make a stand (*antistanta*) and bring down the stroke
> of Calamity upon one's soul is a dread alternative. (1095-
> 7)[21]

Then, less than ten lines later, Creon voices the final military
estimate that appears within the play as he decides to yield
to Teiresias' warnings:

> Alas! But, though it's hard, I turn now from my heart's
> resolve and do it. One must not fight a hopeless fight
> (*dysmachêteon*) against necessity. (1105-6)

Still partially, but at least in some measure, Creon in these
words recognizes at last that the business of personal and
civic conduct involves more complex forces and less simple
procedures than the kind of ordonnance at which he had
aimed.

In summary, then, it is apparent that the iterative military imagery relates in great measure to Creon as do the images of the other two sequences considered in this chapter. They serve to shade in the quality of his thought: concrete in vision and expression, admiring the orderly, impatient of what cannot be brought under an elementary, direct kind of order. And this sequence of images serves also to suggest very early in the play, and then progressively to confirm, the system of government to which Creon's kind of attitude and action may lead under stress—namely, to a rigorous autocracy. Moreover, up until at least the middle of the Haimon scene (to about 683 or perhaps not until the exchange in 733-40) this is a revelation of qualities and attitudes in Creon which to a great extent lie beneath the surface of intellectual honesty, everyday common sense, and general respectability. Thus in the lecture to Haimon (639-80) the poet does not offer simply one *or* another interpretation of Creon's attitude but affords us instead several levels of meaning and evaluation simultaneously. At this point in the action Creon is the master of the action. He has the allegiance and general approval of the Chorus. And it seems, dramatically at least, that he may be in the right; whereas Antigone, for all her lofty appeals to divine law, is likely to seem self-centered, highly emotional, and overly forward, especially in view of the conventions limiting feminine enterprise in fifth century Athens. The dramatic peripety is still to come and, with it, the full recognition that Creon has been terribly short-sighted and wrong in his conception of his subjects and in the means by which he tries to control Antigone and Haimon. So, in his lecture to his son we find Creon still presented with a specious attractiveness of a sort: his appeal to filial duty, the call for an higher allegiance to civic good as above one's private interests, the familiar notes he may have struck in respect to the duty of military training, etc. But foreshadowed in Antigone's opening speeches and later latent within Creon's own language are the ominous suggestions which we have observed, and these prepare in a most functional manner for the dramatic revelation and the catastrophe. By this deeply ironic, two-level manner of presentation we are, I feel, reminded that the things in which Creon genuinely believes—civic order, filial duty, discipline, the duty of the individual to the social organization—are genuine qualities and true necessaries for men in terms of society. We are not, that is, led to deny the values or the needs, but we are required to suspect their self-sufficiency, their validity when appealed to as ends in themselves and not treated as parts of a larger moral complex which, in the play, definitely includes the value of the individual person and religious values.[22]

## *Men* : *Brutes* :: *Gods* : *Men*
### THE IMAGERY OF ANIMALS AND THE CONTROL OF ANIMALS

The images drawn from animals and their control in the *Antigone* appear with greater frequency than either the monetary or military images, and their implications for the valuation and direction of human beings extend more deeply. The extensive interactions within this image pattern introduce into the total structure a basic relationship between the animal, the human, and the suprahuman and show it to be part of the moral order of the tragic universe. In briefest terms this relation can be diagrammed as the ratio which forms the heading of this section: as men are to brutes so are the gods to men. In the developments of the animal imagery from which this ratio can be extracted, the play makes clear not only the superiority of gods to men but also, and equally emphatically, the inaccuracy of that kind of human arithmetic which transfers the terms within the ratio and leads a man to set himself up as mentally and morally superior to his fellow men. In a sense, Creon breaks the ratio and is broken by it. Or one might also say that the sequence of animal images very concretely embodies Creon's species of intellectual and moral *hybris*, the human pride that assumes it can judge finally for itself all problems that face it and so brings retribution from the gods.

To observe specifically the manner in which the animal imagery is developed to work these implications integrally

26

into the tragedy, let us again first consider Creon's employment of the imagery and then those developments which show the limitations of his attitude. In the first episode, for example, Creon is made to link, but not to interrelate, the main terms of the pattern, for here, when Creon first learns of the token burial given Polyneices' corpse by an unknown agent, he rejects vehemently the suggestion that the gods may have had a part in the deed. He suspects political dissatisfaction as the motive and voices his suspicion first in an image from draft animals:

> It cannot be [the gods]. No, from the first certain men of the city, chafing at the edict, have muttered against me and tossed their heads in secret. They have not kept their necks duly under the yoke to accept my sway. (289-92)

The image of the yoke for tyranny had been worked frequently by Aeschylus—for example, extended into a magnificent symbol of the Persian system of government in the *Persians* (esp. 189-98) and joined repeatedly with the threat of enslavement in the *Seven Against Thebes*. The yoke is also used in the Theognidean elegies (e.g. 847-50) as a fixed symbol of the right procedure for oligarchic and autocratic governments in keeping the commons down. But such parallels in themselves do not demand a hard and fast political signification for the particular image, apart from its context. Definitely instrumental in the effect and value of Creon's image is the way in which it is presented partly by indirection, so that one seems to be invited to hurry past it to the extended and vivid personification of money which follows immediately (293-303). The poet does not, or does not yet, permit us a simple choice between the rightness or wrongness of Creon's conduct. Dramatically, Creon still seems a fairly rational, if somewhat sententious, leader, sincere in his attitude and probably more right than not. But the application of the draft-animal-yoking image to the citizens opens a potential suggestion that Creon's way is the tyrannical way, the way of slavery.

27

This somewhat veiled suggestion both prepares for the future course of action and is actualized in the subsequent progress of the tragedy. It is gradually strengthened as there appears in Creon's language the repeated suggestion that he views his fellow men, especially those who oppose him, as brutishly and slavishly his inferiors. Thus when Antigone has confronted him without a sign of yielding and has made her speech about the unwritten laws of the gods, Creon replies with a series of threatening parables, including the following:

> I have seen spirited horses broken just by a small bridle.
> No, there is no room for pride when one is one's neigh-
> bor's slave. (477-9) [23]

Polyneices is, in Creon's phrase, "one who came to feed on kindred blood" (201-2), and it is with particular concreteness and vehemence that Creon speaks of Polyneices' body as now fit animal carrion,

> a corpse for birds and dogs to eat [and leave] mangled
> for all to see. (205-6) [24]

The corpse of Polyneices exposed to the beasts is, in a sense, a basic image of situation for the play and one which is integrated closely with the verbal imagery.

But there is another factor also in the examples just considered; the direct juxtaposition of notions of slavery with the bestial imagery. The mentions of slaves and slavery form in themselves a suggestive minor sequence, which, because of its close relation to the yoke and bridle images, may profitably be considered with them. In his first speech when Creon describes Polyneices' crimes and concludes by branding him as one who has come "to feed on kindred blood and lead the remnant into slavery" (202), the mention of enslavement is climactic and presumably is one of the strongest of his charges against Polyneices. This may indicate for the play the degree of active antipathy carried within the characterization of a person as an enslaver. Yet later, as we have noted, Creon offers Antigone a metaphor of a slave together with one of the bridle by way of threatening example, and in these particular examples we get some suggestion of the kind of obedience he expects to gain. In the same scene Antigone insists on Polyneices' right to pious burial by urging specifically that he was *not* a slave (517). Her implication is clear, especially in its proximity to Creon's threat: namely, that Creon has treated the corpse as though it were a "slave-thing" and so has assumed an undue attitude of superiority over free men and relatives. We may look on farther also, to Creon's final argument with Haimon, where Creon in anger virtually rejects his son's filial status:

> HA. If you were not my father, I should say you were not wise.
> CR. You woman's slave, don't try to wheedle me! (755-6)

Thus it is without exception Creon whose metaphors tend to reduce other people, and finally his own son, to the level of slaves. Ironically, it is Creon himself who in a fine burst of rhetoric first stresses the hostility due to the enslaver. This progressive use of terms of enslavement is paralleled and extended by the further animal comparisons which Creon employs.

When Ismene makes her second entrance she, too, draws an image of this order from Creon:

> You too, Ismene, who like an adder have lurked in the house and stealthily sucked out my blood; and all the while I did not realize that I was raising twin plagues and revolutions for my throne. Come speak out. . . . (531-3)[25]

At the end of this scene, as Creon orders that Antigone and Ismene be led off, animal imagery echoes again, in an expression packed with several levels of meaning:

> Take them in servants. From now on they must be women, not let to range at large (*mêd' aneimenas*). For, to be sure, even the brave try to run when they see the

lord Hades [viz. Death] already close on them. (578-81)

We are given here, in a keyed phrase, a term used especially of animals dedicated to a god and let roam free.[26] The image is reinforced by mention of the specific god, and this reference has functional values from the wider context that also bear on the image. A few lines previously Antigone had proclaimed her total allegiance to the nether world (559-60); in the next scene Creon very explicitly stresses the folly of such self-dedication to Hades (777-80). The dedicatory image in 578-81 forms, as it were, a bridge between these two expressions, even as it compresses in itself the antithetical views of the two chief characters. In the subsequent action, Antigone's self-dedication to Hades, which is here the object of Creon's contempt and disbelief, becomes more and more tragically real, being a theme which is developed in the imagery of marriage. Conversely, Creon's sense of superiority over his fellows, which is also reflected in this image, is shown to be less and less valid, even as the prerogative of his kingly office.

There is one further animal image used by Creon prior to the catastrophe which we should observe, for it appears at the particular point where he makes his final decision regarding Antigone prior to the "recognition." The expression again is brief, a single word which because of the previous manifestations of Creon's attitude in similar terms serves as a telling sign at this point. In describing the living entombment that he plans for Antigone, Creon says he will have left for her only enough *fodder* as will permit her to sustain life and so keep pollution from the city (775-6).[27] And in the word we are reminded surely of the implications of radical a-morality in Creon's position, even as he retains a certain caution about the higher moral governance of the gods.

The other images of the sequence sharpen the implications of the images we have observed and show clearly the fundamental errors of this aspect of Creon's attitude whereby he recurrently asserts his authority in terms of the superiority of humanity over animal nature. Certain elements of the odes are particularly instrumental in extending the significance of the animal imagery in its several functions. It is entirely appropriate for the elders of "many charioted Thebes" that images of driving and racing should be frequent in the odes of this play. We shall not attempt to consider all the appearances but instead be selective with an eye to structural significance. The imagery of the odes is generally more intricately compact and is treated more fully in a subsequent chapter. Here I wish to direct attention particularly to four developments within the odes that are of special significance in setting the major values of the total animal pattern.

(1) The first ode, the Parodos (100-54), as the Chorus enters the play, contains the first significant use of animal imagery in the play. Besides the conflict of the eagle and snake developed at some length (110-26), the ode includes a series of images from charioteering and the racetrack. For example, Ares has been "the trusty trace-horse" bringing victory to the Thebans (139-40). The Argive host, or its representative Capaneus, had nearly raced victoriously to the "finish wire" when Zeus struck down (131-3).[28] And in the first strophe, the sun in semi-personification "drives in head-long flight with galling curb the white-shielded hero from Argos" (106-9).[29] None of these images is expanded or drawn in clear detail. In fact, their very lack of visual distinctness and the way in which the driving or racing images rise and submerge and shift quickly into other images add to the confusion and terror of the conflict and to the sense of dark danger just passed. Yet in these initial driving images we have an observable balance set up for Creon's final image of the same sort. In the ode the gods are the drivers, and this is the recognition to which Creon finally comes when he says near the end of the play:

> Now surely some god struck down on my head, constraining me with great weight. He drove me into wild ways, overturning my joy so that it is trampled down.
> (1272-5)[30]

When Creon does, after the catastrophe, come to view himself as the driven rather than the driver, we get a poignant reflection of the limitations of his former view as expressed through the animal imagery. More fundamental, however, in the tragedy as a whole is the manner in which the driving images at the start of the play and at its close show men to be under the gods' sway, instead of crediting to one man the right to yoke and bridle others.

(2) In the second ode (Stasimon I, 332-75) additional basic propositions are offered in terms of the animal imagery that oppose the kind of self-elevation for which Creon has used this imagery. They more or less draw up a framework in which his use of animal imagery is to be apprehended. Antistrophe *a* and the final lines of the preceding strophe portray man's prowess in subduing and putting to his use the earth and its creatures. The yoke is specifically mentioned (351). But when the ode passes on to man's control of himself and his fellow men, the yoke is conspicuously absent. For human governance we have this instead:

> Words also and wind-swift thought has man *taught himself* and the dispositions which regulate cities. (354-6)

This ode is by no means the simple glorification of human accomplishment for which later-day humanists seem often to take it. The dangerous quality of man's freedom is very strongly stated (365ff.), and a correlation of human with divine law is required (368-9). Yet in the final two strophes the picture of man as his own teacher and as free, except from the gods, is in telling contrast to the picture of man's domination over brute nature in the first two strophes. It is also in significant contrast to Creon's closely preceding characterization of his own rule and of citizens of his state by a draft-animal-yoking image (289-92).

In the contrasts which their animal imagery offers to Creon's recurrent uses of animal terms these first two odes establish strong normative implications which, as was suggested earlier, may be stated as a symbolic ratio. As brutes are inferior to men, so are men inferior to the gods. This is a true ratio in which transfer of an inside and an outside term is faulty intellection. Men's elementary and qualitative superiority over animals is not paralleled in the relation of men with each other. It does not provide a true basis for one to imagine that he is radically superior to his fellows. Near the end of the tragedy Creon himself is finally made to express some recognition of these facts, when he states his error and his inferiority to the gods in the terms of the bridled and driven relation which he had faultily applied to the relation of his fellows to his own authority.

(3) Further images in the play help to mark the terms of this quadripartite ratio. So in the fourth ode (Stasimon III, 781-99), the ode on Eros, the strange incontestable power of the god over men is expressed with a metaphor from the driving of horses:

> Truly you make swerve upon ($\pi\alpha\rho\alpha\sigma\pi\hat{\alpha}s$) ruin the just man's consenting heart. (791-2)[31]

Then at the end of the ode, caught in a position of divided loyalties (one in which the gods seem to them to be at work), the Chorus applies a similar metaphor to itself:

> Now I, I too, am *carried outside the track* of lawful institutions (*thesmôn*), as I see these things. (800-1)[32]

In both cases, as in the first ode, there is an obvious suggestion that forces greater than men are the drivers to whose directions men must submit.

(4) Then again in the fifth ode (Stasimon IV, 944-87) there is a series of yoking and animal images (947, 955, 985). These images, as I shall show more fully, relate closely to the major distinctions which we have observed as present within the total image pattern, and they protest, indirectly, against the action Creon has taken in sending Antigone to living entombment. But the bearing of this ode in the dramatic structure is particularly complicated. Its images need to be observed closely in rich context of the ode itself, and this is best done in a separate treatment.[33]

For the sequence of animal images as a whole it is significant that almost no one besides Creon uses this form of imagery, except the Chorus in the odes. One telling exception, to which we shall recur, is Teiresias' account of his augury (999-1004; cf. 1021-2). Even animal nature has been confounded to some extent by Creon's actions but still it manages to testify against him. In some measure, that is, we are given here in the scene of peripety a specific contradiction to Creon's previous use of animal imagery to debase others. There are two lesser exceptions in the Messenger speech toward the close of the play, one of which quotes Creon.[34] And as they both catch up, again with a kind of retroactive irony, Creon's recurrent use of animal comparisons prior to the catastrophe, they may fittingly conclude this portion of our survey of the dominant image patterns which relate most closely to him. The first of these closing echoes in the animal pattern is in the description of Haimon as he faces his father in the death vault:

> Glaring at him with wild eyes (*agriois ossoisi paptênas*),
> he spat in his face and answered nothing. (1231-2)[35]

There is, one may feel, a connective overtone of particularly bitter irony as the son in subhuman rage glares now on the father who has been so prone to assign bestial characteristics to others but who would now, too late, make atonement. The other instance is still more indirect and keenly edged if we are attentive to the vibrancies of the imagery. It is in the description of Creon's progress to Antigone's prison. Hearing cries from the rocky vault, Creon is reported by the Messenger to have lamented and then to have said, παιδός με σαίνει φθόγγος (most literally: My son's voice wags me greeting) (1214). It has seemed safest to most to regard the metaphor as thoroughly generalized, as meaning simply "greets"; for the verb, *sainô*, though used originally of dogs wagging their tails, often enough seems to denote fawning and flattery and joyful greeting or gladdening. If the term here were taken as only and entirely concrete in its basic sense, the effect would be crass, and the harshness with which it would set the breach between appearance and reality, both in Creon's former appraisal of his son and in his situation at this minute, might seem too bitterly ironic even for Sophocles. But this is a question not just of denotations but more of connotations, of the multiple effects and active overtones aroused by a word of general tenor (here: greets) which includes a more particular, latent vehicle (wags at, fawns upon), with both elements interacting as a result of context. So regarded, the particular ironic implications of the canine term are a functional and valid part of the expression wherein Creon speaks of his son for the first time since their angry and fatal parting.[36] Actually, retroactive irony of this sort, turning for the most part back on Creon from terms and ideas which he has launched quite differently, is characteristic of many of the images toward the end of the play. And here it would seem that, even as he has Creon "unconsciously" use this term related to his former, catastrophic manner of judgment, the poet has chosen just the right term to tie the expression into the larger tragic structure. It is immaterial whether the poet himself performed this by a subconscious "Freudian slip" or with the heightened awareness always attributable to exceptional masters of language.

# CHAPTER III · THE LARGER TRAGIC PERSPECTIVE IN THREE SUPPORTING IMAGE PATTERNS

THE questions of motivation, valuation, and control, both private and public, which are developed by the major image sequences are set within a kind of total order whose bearing extends from the bestial to the divine but within which man is required to find his way by a difficult process of trial and error and suffering. In this process, the pragmatic, orderly, and what is real to the eye may, we come to see, be tragically deceptive and so lead to a destructive wrenching in the final order, and this in turn brings retribution as it reasserts its ultimate validity. So far we are describing the converging patterns of attitude and insight afforded by the three dominant image sequences in cooperation with the plot. Three lesser image patterns function to discover the facts of the tragic system of things as it operates in the *Antigone*, and they do so by calling upon internal, emotional kinds of experience, as in the marriage imagery, and upon more external and almost cosmic situations, as in the imagery of the sea. They are closely integrated to the play's structure and, by the peculiar power of metaphor, evoke for it perceptions that are simultaneously specific and extensive. Thus from one point of view the recurrent imagery of marriage, disease, and the sea gives particularity to the expression of such universal issues as the conflict of body and soul, evil, and the relation of human and suprahuman modes of value which are part of the tragic conflict in the work. Yet in another sense these images extend the general implications of the dramatic conflict. For they assist in setting the particular plot in a perspective of universally familiar elements of experience, and in so doing they help the particular events of the plot to be felt as carrying far-reaching elements of moral and religious experience.

36

## The Marriage Motif

The imagery of marriage, especially as it is used in close connection with death, is a fairly prominent element in the overall structure of the play and brings to it insights of both emotional and religious import, while also serving to express dramatic character and motivation. A high degree of tension achieved within the recurrent images coupling death and marriage embodies, with poignance and some of the force of paradox, the conflicting claims of body and spirit, life and death which underlie the tragic conflict. In these respects the imagery has a close parallel in *Romeo and Juliet*.[1] No simple solution is offered for the claims, any more than the play as a whole offers a painless panacea for evil or a codified sailing manual for the hidden perils of life.

Creon first gives expression to the combined image, as he warns his son away from Antigone:

Don't lose your head, my son, for the pleasure of a woman. Be sure of this, she makes a cold piece in your arms, when the bed-fellow in your home is a villainess. For what greater sore can there be than a loved one who is evil? No, spit her out, and as though she were your enemy *let the girl go to Hades and find a husband.* (648-54)[2]

In the next episode, immediately after the ode on Love's paradoxical powers, the Chorus catches up the fusion of marriage and death, but with sympathy, as it sees Antigone enter:

No longer can I check the tears which well up as now I see Antigone passing to that bridal chamber (*thalamon*) where all find sleep at last (*pagkoitên*). (802-5)[3]

In the lyric kommos which follows, Antigone sounds the same paradox, and variants of it, repeatedly and pathetically—for example:

Look at me, citizens of my father's land, treading my last road, looking at the sun a last time, and never again.

37

> Now Hades who lays all to sleep (*pagkoitas*) leads me still alive to the shore of Acheron. No usual marriage hymns for me; no song for the bride has sounded outside my door. By Acheron I shall be wed. (806-16)[4]

The concluding stanza of the kommos repeats the image of the marriage hymns (which she lacks) together with those of the last journey and last view of the sun. And the feeling that her imprisonment is both an entombment and a sort of bridal event is sustained in the intervening Niobe simile (823-33), especially in the last word of the last line—"Most like her some god lays me to rest (*kateunazei*)."

The external basis of the ironic or paradoxical imagery of death as a bridal in this semi-lyric passage is obviously that girls of Antigone's age should normally expect marriage and festive epithalamia in place of imprisonment or living entombment. The tone of the kommos, in which Antigone is now likely to seem overly repetitive and even flagrantly self-pitying, most certainly was deepened and intensified by accompanying music. It has been suggested that the music for this dirge-like passage may have furthered the contrast between dramatic fact and normal expectation by recalling the musical modes characteristic of marriage hymns, and the costuming and stage pageant may have given a similar visible symbolization to the polar tension offered in the imagery.[5] But whether or not this was so, the nuptial imagery here has a closer role in the full context of the play than simply to arouse pathos for Antigone on the basis of a maiden's normal expectation at this time of life. Thus after the kommos, near the close of the episode Antigone repeats the marriage motif twice more. In her last long speech before her final exit, an often questioned and expurgated speech, she states her final allegiance to her family as above any husband she might have had:

> O tomb, my bridal chamber (*nympheion*). O eternal caverned home where I go to find my own, of whom the greatest number have perished and been received by Persephone among the dead (891-4). . . . Now like a

captive in his hands he [Creon] has me led off—one
who has not known bridal bed or bridal hymns, nor has
had due share of marriage and the care of children. No,
thus barren of friends and ill-fated, I go still alive to the
caverns of the dead. (916-20)[6]

A maiden who should expect marriage, she goes to a fate
that is only a "bridal" in the most ironic sense, the sleep with
Death. But although the prospect draws, it seems, real fear
and anguish from her, she is scornful of other alternatives
and makes her choice of death in preference to the customary
marital affections which she might have had. In the episode as
a whole, that is, the repetition of death and marriage allusions
together does not only generate pathos; it is part of the
portrayal of Antigone's rise above the passive reception of
sympathy.

At the same time, the reiterated images coupling death and
marriage provide "motivation," or make emotional preparation, for Haimon's later actions. And this is accomplished
in great measure poetically, by imagery and verbal overtones,
without complicating the concentrated dramatic action with
a developed erotic sub-plot.[7] The death-as-a-bridal imagery,
as a matter of fact, next appears in the Messenger's report
of the double catastrophe at Antigone's prison, where verbal
emphasis reinforces the preceding dramatic economy by a
four-fold repetition. Here the Messenger begins his description of events at the prison as follows:

We then approached toward the maiden's stone-strewn,
Death's-bridal cavern. But from a distance we heard a
voice wailing loudly at that fatal, unhallowed marriage
chamber (akteriston amphi pastada). (1204-7)[8]

He tells then how they found that Antigone had hung herself
and that Haimon was with her,

Embracing her body, hanging on her, crying aloud for
his bride below (eunês tês katô), her destruction, the
works of his father and his own ill-fated bed. (1223-5)[9]

Then at the conclusion, having described how Haimon first turned against his father and then killed himself, the Messenger reports:

> Corpse embracing corpse, he lies there, gaining his nuptial rites (*ta nymphika telê*), poor youth, in the house of Hades. (1240-1)

Again we find the backward-turning structural irony in this final appearance of the marital imagery, for we recall that it is Creon who introduces the death-as-a-bridal motif into the play by urging that Haimon let Antigone "go and find a husband in Hades." But to some extent there is here also a different and deeper kind of judgment, developed at least in partial form.

To some extent, that is, we all tend to judge actions by their ends and in the final cause, as it were, feel that we find essential meanings of acts in progress. So in some measure the messengered union of Haimon with Antigone is a terminally symbolic action which gives to the lines of action they each chose in a divisive and frustrating situation some of the understanding and affirmation which can come from accomplished goal.[10] Some sort of life after death is definitely asserted as a religious fact (or perhaps better, hypothesis) for the play, both in the primary dramatic issue of burial and in Teiresias' eschatological pronouncements (esp. 1070-6). But, while we are offered recognition of these matters, it is not a simple, unclouded recognition, and we should be wrong to read into the play a final glorious transfiguration for Haimon and Antigone, such as Sophocles could, when he wanted to, create in magnificent style—viz. the *Oedipus at Colonus*. When the nuptial imagery, even including the eschatological hypotheses of the play, is viewed in the total context and together with the emphases provided by the action, the "promise" of spiritual union provided by the linked deaths of Antigone and Haimon is a faint, heavily over-shadowed promise, under a heavy feeling of waste. The major impact provided by their deaths is tragic destruction rather than guaranteed bliss. But it is just in this building of severe tension between different realms of essential life that the fused imagery of marriage and death has its fullest bearing within the play. In the intense expression which the recurrent images give to the interlaced claims of body and spirit, this sequence puts before us in emotional terms the range of attitudes and values (material and spiritual, reasoned and intuited, pragmatic and final) within which the temporal actions of the characters are offered for consideration and judgment.

## Images of Disease and Cure

While the imagery of marriage is somewhat ambiguous about the man-god relationship in postmortal conditions, the other two supporting sequences are nearly as explicit in setting its bearing for life as is the animal pattern. Evil, cosmic and moral, is the special burden of the disease and cure images, and for this they have a traditional basis going back to Homer. The expression of almost any adverse condition as a *nosos* (disease, diseased state) can be found in Greek poetry. In the Homeric epics it is almost always conceived as a visitation from an angry deity, but in Greek tragedy the idea of a *nosos* seems to be transferred often to distress and sorrow or to mental disorder and to causes of great commotion, without necessary supernatural connection. In the *Antigone* the image utilizes the range between these possibilities. The pattern formed is not a major one on the basis of frequency or of detailed exploitation. But in the few main lines which it offers, the sequence recurrently relates evil to the early religious or cosmic conception of disease, and from this it points up a more genuinely tragic conception of infectious moral evil and resultant suffering.

The first appearance verges on the Homeric type of view. The Guard, in describing how he and his fellows were obstructed from guarding the corpse of Polyneices by a sudden windstorm, concludes his description as follows:

... it filled the plain, tearing off all the tresses of the groves, and the wide air was choked full. We closed our eyes and endured the divine plague (*theian noson*). (419-21)

41

But Creon has already refused any suggestion of divine intervention on behalf of Polyneices (278-89), and the Guard here, at least on the surface, seems chiefly to be trying to make his story vivid and impressive. The word next appears in the Haimon scene, used in a somewhat more human, psychological sense by Creon. Haimon and Creon are in open argument:

> HA. No, I would not urge reverence (*eusebein*) of evil-doers.
> CR. But is not the girl gripped by a sickness (*nosos*) of that sort? (731-2)[11]

What Creon means, of course, is that Antigone is deranged in paying attention to enemies of the state like Polyneices. But there is here a suggestion that Creon is deliberately made to deride a religious notion, for Haimon's term *eusebein* is regularly and primarily a religious term for the display of reverence and piety, though, to be sure, it may also signify general "respect."

This is significant, for when the imagery of disease next appears, used in an extended form by Teiresias, the whole city has been gripped by a plague arising from Creon's impiety. The gods are offended. Creon is now the one who needs to seek a cure. The blind seer is explicit on these points:

> The city sickens (*nosei*) thus from your attitude (*tês sês ek phrenos*). For the altars of the city and of the private homes, one and all, have been infected (*plêreis*) . . . by carrion from the son of Oedipus. And therefore the gods no longer accept prayers and sacrifices from us (1015-20).[12] . . . Yet for all men it is common to err. But, when an error is made, that man is no longer witless or unblest who applies a cure for (*akeitai*) the trouble into which he has fallen and does not remain all sluggish (*akinêtos*). (1023-7)[13]

A little later in the same scene Teiresias again directs the disease imagery to criticize Creon's attitude (1052), much as Creon had used it to stress Antigone's mental derangement. As the seer uses the images, we have Creon not only as one who is internally infected or mentally deranged but as a source of "infection" extending to the whole city and spreading even beyond the city through carrion birds carrying the taint (1080-3). The more simple notion in the Guard's expression, that trouble comes from the gods, has been sublimated into more substantial conception wherein the errors and sins of men are self-engendered pestilences that spread pollution under the wrathful oversight of the gods.[14]

The following ode (Stasimon v, 1115-54) evokes the religious associations of *nosos* still again. Taking hope from Creon's change of heart following Teiresias' warnings, the Chorus invokes the god Dionysus and in the second strophe calls upon him to bring health back to the city:

> Now come with cleansing (healing, *katharsios*) foot over the slope of Parnassus or from across the moaning strait, now when all the city is held by a violent plague (*biaias epi nosou*). (1140-5)

In the play the actual "cure" takes place through the more terrible and real process of tragic retribution and tragic waste rather than at the hands of a *deus ex machina*. This we get in other terms than medical imagery, except perhaps for connotations in one of Creon's final laments, where the nautical and purgative imagery overlap:

> Alas! Alas! O harbor of Hades hard to cleanse and to appease (*dyskathartos Haidou limên*). (1284)

Here the adjective, directly linked to Hades' port but indirectly linked with the god of Death, may connote that he is indeed a god severe in his methods of purging such pollution as Creon has generated.

But even without this final reference, it is apparent that imagery of disease as it is developed in the play supports on a smaller scale the patterns of the other image sequences, particularly those built with the animal imagery and the imagery of the sea. Like them it relates the human action to the "action" of the gods, which, though not visible on stage, is shown to be the final determinant in human welfare. Like the other images also, the lines of perspective offered by this sequence show that men are not viewed as freed from responsibility because of the gods' preeminence. They help instead to set a situation in which men must carefully direct their actions, lest spreading harm they destroy not so much themselves as others.

## Images of the Sea and Sailing

From the standpoint of frequency the nautical imagery is one of the major sequences of the play, and its development is only slightly less thorough than that of the animal imagery, especially as a symbolic vehicle. In part the nautical imagery helps to express the accomplishments of human ingenuity and also some of the need for cooperative endeavor. At the same time the sea with its storms and depth and violence is employed to give concrete embodiment to the workings of the gods as the great and elemental moral forces of the universe, beyond man's complete understanding or control but fundamental to his success and welfare. These symbolic or semi-symbolic values are to an appreciable extent common to imagery of the sea in other Greek poetry. The significance of the imagery in the *Antigone*, that is, arises from the functional employment of such familiar conceits as the sea of life, the ship of state, and storms of trouble. There is every evidence to believe that for the Greeks these images were not mere clichés but, because of the people's close dependence on the sea, had genuine representational and imaginative value to express feelings of aspiration, difficult achievement, and the existence of greater forces limiting human endeavor. Thus at a rather elementary level man's conquest of the sea and his ability to sail over it are, in the play, a recurrent and vital symbol of daring and resourcefulness: for example, 334-7 in Stasimon I, the victory of man's daring over the sea and its storms; 615-16 in Stasimon II, man's "wide-ranging hope" (*ha polyplagktos elpis*) calling up the image of the mariner on the seas;[15] and 953-5 in Stasimon IV, where the black ships are one of four embodiments of human power and accomplishment. In parallel fashion the great range and power of the gods Eros and Dionysus find concrete description in their crossing of the sea: 785 in Stasimon III and 1117-19 in Stasimon V.

The troubles and dangers of life, private and civil, are given reiterated expression in storms of the sea and the image of life as a voyage. And here the development of the imagery is somewhat more subtle and more closely integrated to the action. Four marine images are shared between Ismene and Antigone, and the associations established by their responsions form fine threads of connection between their respective attitudes in their two chief scenes and also link them into the destiny of their family under the power of the gods. The first of these images is close to the opening of the play. Having been called aside by Antigone for some secret purpose still unknown to her, Ismene asks:

> What is it? Clearly your words are dark and stormy (*kalchainous' epos*). (20)

"Dark and troublous, like a stormy sea" her term implies.[16] Later Antigone in reply also uses an expression in which we may feel a nautical basis:

> Fear not for me. Steer straight (*eksorthou*) your own fate. (83)[17]

Neither of these images is compelling in itself, but the significant and reiterated responsion when next the sisters meet suggests that as part of the emotional fabric of this opening scene we have Antigone embarking on a perilous voyage where Ismene is afraid to venture. The catching up of this suggestion occurs in the second episode, when Antigone has been detected and the sisters are made to confront each other before Creon. In her first speech upon entrance, in reply to Creon's question of whether she took part in the burial, Ismene answers at once:

> I did the deed, even though she rows by my side (*homorothei*). I share the charge and I accept the guilt. (536-7)[18]

45

And when Antigone refuses her a share, Ismene again voices her wish for partnership in the terms which had figured in their initial division:

> But now in the evils which beset you, I am not ashamed to make my voyage with you (*ksymploun*) in your suffering. (540-1)

In the choral ode which follows, the plight of both sisters is set within the fateful history of their family, the house of Labdacus. The sea imagery is instrumental in the expression of this connection, and here it rises to its most forceful and extended appearance in the play to include also the mysterious and overwhelming power of the gods over men (582-97).

But alongside the images of the sea of life and its storms as they are applied to and by Antigone for her line of action, there is early in the play a strong and sustained employment of sea imagery by Creon. It is by this that we perhaps first have signaled to us the prominence of this pattern for the play and are first directed to its major bearings: the obligations of human endeavor in the context of the elemental moral forces of the universe. In Creon's intitial speech the image of the ship of state is used to bracket his claims to leadership and obedience, just before he announces his edict:

> Gentlemen, the gods have righted safe (*ôrthôsan*) once more the affairs of the city after tossing them in great surges (162-3). . . . Now to me the man who has the task of guiding (*euthynôn*) a whole city and who does not fasten on the best counsels, but from fear keeps his lips locked, this man has always seemed the basest sort. And any man who reckons a friend or kinsman as greater than his fatherland, this man I count of no account (178-83). . . . For I am sure of this, that it is the city which carries us safe and that only while she sails steady under us (*tautês epi pleontes orthês*) do we make real friends. (188-90)[19]

This sustained image of the ship of state is a traditional and respected figure. The fact has effect in the initial presentation of Creon as a somewhat sententious but generally rational and acceptable proponent of conservative political views. A tone is established which carries over into the proclamation of his edict so that the impiety of the edict, which is to prove a major cause of Creon's undoing, is reserved for development in the course of the play.

As a part of the revelation that occurs finally in the Teiresias scene, the image of the ship of state appears for the only other time in the play. As Teiresias enters, Creon asks:

Cr. What is it, ancient Teiresias? something new?
Te. I shall teach you, and be sure you obey the prophet.
Cr. To be sure, I have not previously avoided your counsel.
Te. For that reason you used to pilot (*enauklêreis*) the city safely. (991-4)

One after another the critical image sequences converge in this scene of recognition and peripety. With this compressed image in this context we are reminded of the dependence upon the gods voiced in Creon's initial statement of the ship-of-state imagery. Their influence upon his pilotage of the state he has meantime been led to ignore, but he is soon to feel again their control of the "sea of life."

The sea imagery in the third ode (Stasimon II), to which we have already referred, is additionally significant in this respect for the emphatic expression it gives to the elemental power of the gods in shaping the course of human events. In the opening strophe of that ode, the specific reference is to the woes of the house of Labdacus, Laius, Oedipus *et al.*:

Fortunate are men who have never tasted of evil. Where once a house has been shaken by the gods, there Calamity (*atê*) works to the full, moving darkly from generation to generation: Just as when a crested wave, driven by the savage sea-winds of Thrace, runs over the nether darkness of the sea and rolls up black sand from the depths; and a low roar sounds from the wind-vexed headlands as they meet the onslaught.

> From times long past I see misery has surged upon
> misery and death in the house of Labdacus.[20] Generation
> frees not generation. Some god dashes them down, and
> there is no release. . . . (582-97)

The dramatic reference is to Antigone and Ismene, and the
imagery appears to have had its point of departure from
Ismene's images in 536 and 541. But as is considered more
fully in the next chapter, the ode as a whole develops from
this image to present a complex awareness of human moral
responsibility and does not leave us simply with an ancestral
curse. There is no explicit reference to Creon, but as Jebb
notes, the words all through are broadly suggestive and ominous.[21] Life, in a major extension of the sea imagery, is a
most mysterious and perilous voyage very much influenced
by divine forces. And with its religio-cosmic view of life
the ode forms an important check-point between Creon's
apparent attitude in his initial use of the ship of state image
(including the gods) and his actual practice in the play. The
latter is crystallized by Teiresias' turning of the same image
against him, for ignoring the gods.

On several other occasions in the play life is regarded as
a voyage. Haimon in the scene following the third ode uses a
sailing simile to try to impress his father with the need of
yielding to better counsel and, by implication, to forces
greater than his own will:

> Even if a man is wise, there is no shame in his still learn-
> ing many things and not being over-taut in his atti-
> tude. . . . In just this way, the man who draws the sheet
> of the sail too taut and never slackens it upsets the boat
> and makes the rest of his voyage top-side down. (710-
> 17)

The prophecy which these lines contain may be felt to be
indirectly applicable to Antigone and Haimon himself, as well
as to Creon, but the fact that it is pointed explicitly as a warning for Creon pulls it into close relation with the three images
just previously considered. Then, at the end of the play, there
appears one last telling nautical metaphor, used by Creon,

that carries an overtone of bitter recognition for the over-self-confidence of his earlier helmsmanship:

O harbor of Death (*Haidou limên*), hard to cleanse.
Why? Why do you destroy me? (1283-5)

Creon's piloting has steered to destruction and death for others, while for him particularly death, though the "harbor" to which all must come as a final destination, bears least promise of a "port" of refuge. Taken in its most visual possibilities, the phrase evidences the wreckage Creon has helped create, if, as Campbell felt, death here presents itself to Creon's mind as a harbor choked and befouled with corpses.[22] But even in its more probable form as a sunken, less visually precise image, "Hades' harbor" here offers a specific and ironic reminder of Creon's former self-assurance, especially in view of the fact that this is the very "god" with whom Creon had expressed himself as being most unconcerned (e.g. 777-80; also 578-81, 654).

The other nautical images in the play are of more limited activity, sharpening or giving sensuous body to individual expressions.[23] In terms of the whole, however, the very frequency of the sea references deepens the emotional and imaginative perspective in which the dramatic action is viewed. None of them seems to open false leads or divert attention away from the major, structural lines of vision which we have seen this sequence develop in coordination with the other master tropes and the plot development. Consequently we may again employ a rough kind of comparative ratio to outline the relationships which the imagery of the sea helps to develop between the visual action and its religio-moral meanings. As nautical accomplishments show men's strength and limitations in respect to the sea's elemental power and mystery, so do the strivings of the characters and their failings show the greatness and weakness of human aspiration and endeavor in a moral universe that is true to experience. Moreover, as the sea's power is often violent and unfathomable, so all causes of all the catastrophic events in the play cannot be simply and directly attributed to Creon. But, as Teiresias helps to point out, the pilot is responsible for getting his sailing directions from the right source. In this crucial respect Creon is at fault, as various elements within and outside this image sequence show.[24]

As one experiences the *Antigone* and becomes aware of the highly organized fabric of issues and insights which it affords, it is literally impossible to determine the values of any single element without regard to the other elements with which it exists and in terms of which it fulfills its artistic function. The imagery of the sea is not an independent unit in the play; nor are any of the image patterns. As we have seen words interact to take on particular vitalities within sequences, so in a sense the image sequences interact and interanimate each other. Thus the imagery of the sea deals with the question of control and guidance as do the military and animal sequences, and the animal imagery treats the man-gods relation no less than does the imagery of the sea. Similarly the imagery of marriage, for example, shares functions with the monetary, military, and animal imagery in depicting the divergent estimates of human nature and motive advanced by Creon, on the one hand, and Antigone and Haimon on the other, and the nautical imagery, especially as used by Ismene, also speaks of basic motivation. One cannot, then, accurately apprehend one sequence without having the others in mind. In the play we progress in time. As the play unfolds, the major image sequences often come together and cross and recross so as to define each other and develop mutual as well as individual lines of insight. This is most striking in the Teiresias scene where five of the six dominant image sequences are brought together to highlight, as it were, the dramatic recognition. In a more subtle instance of this interdependence, the sixth sequence, the marriage imagery, is not caught up until near the end when Haimon's death is messengered, and there after the catastrophe it provides an ironic, inward recognition which is closely paralleled by the final echoes of the animal, monetary, and nautical imagery. These and other reciprocal relations between the image patterns have been illustrated in some measure already in the discussion of the various sequences. It may profit also to consider the temporal sequence of the image patterns in relation to each other and the plot by means of the appended chart (pp. 120-1). The juxtapositions, overlappings, and concentrations of the dominant imagery are apparent there. One of our chief concerns in the chapters that follow will be the close and meaningful interrelation between the dominant imagery and the other elements of the total structure. It will be seen there more adequately as we progressively widen our inspection of the context within which the image patterns function.

# CHAPTER IV · IMAGERY AND
# STRUCTURE IN THE ODES

THE six choral odes of the *Antigone* present more complex, highly imaginative, and intricate expression than the dialogue portions of the play. Critical analysis is consequently complicated, and the techniques of translation and paraphrase are even less satisfactory in revealing the emotive and connotative richness of meaning in the poetry. At the same time the odes of the play have their being within its structure. Their functions are part of a larger unity. There is no one of the odes which can be dismissed as a casual interpiece, an external and somewhat irrelevant "curtain." Therefore some of the main elements already considered in the total structure provide guides for the understanding of the odes. And as poetic expression the odes are not different in kind from the iambic and semi-lyric portions of the play. The difference, apart from metrical forms and mode of dramatic presentation, is one of degree in poetic qualities and techniques. The odes employ more images more forcefully in constructions which are more elliptical. They compress more elements of meaning more intensely into a smaller compass, and the precision by which they achieve their planned effects is less a matter of logic, or is less denotatively single, than is the case in the iambic dialogue of the play.

Here I have selected only three of the odes for detailed consideration, Stasima I, II, and IV. These, I believe, not only are the most complex and so most requiring of close analysis; they also have the closest bearing on the central meanings of the tragedy. For they express the deep and tangled issues and problems of value which the tragedy raises partly within and partly over and above the immediate conflict of wills. For the other odes this study has little in the way of particular insight to offer beyond what has been presented in other parts of the discussion. But for all the odes I would urge two general principles of interpretation. First, attention to the imagery of the odes and the detail of their verbal expression helps to throw light upon the internal organization of meaning and so to permit a close approach to their rich significances as poems. Secondly, such attention also serves to show more fully their relationships to the larger poem of which they are only parts. The general themes and broader emotional effects of the odes may seem generally clear enough, especially if one regards the action as the thing. But such a view leaves out much of the evidence of the odes themselves and, so, much of their proper bearing for the tragedy.

## Stasimon I (332-75)

The initial statement voices in itself elements of paradox which form the basis of the ode's structure:

πολλὰ τὰ δεινὰ κοὐδὲν ἀνθρώπου δεινότερον πέλει·
(Wonders are many, and none more awesome than man.)

The repetition of the key words, *deina . . . deinoteron*, forms a strong emphasis and opens a range of possible meanings: fearsome and marvelous, potent and strange, mighty and resourceful, wonderful but also terrifying.[1] Danger is as much present as wonder, especially as there may be felt here an allusion to Aeschylus' vivid parallel strophe on the elemental forces of terror in the world (*deina deimatôn achê*) in the *Choephori*.[2] Potency and effective force are aspects of the meaning, so that the line suggests a great active capability as within man by nature and presents this as not simply wonderful or simply dangerous but as both.

The ode develops concretely the multiple connotations opened up by the first line. The first pair of strophes and most of strophe *beta* picture man's wonderful daring and skill in putting the earth and its creatures to his use (332-52) and in developing language, modes of social living, and medicine (353-64). Then in the final antistrophe the element of danger which has been suggested in the opening is caught up explicitly and shown to be a part of that ever-resourceful capacity which distinguishes man:

With skill beyond belief and inventive art he moves now
to evil and now to good. When he weaves together
(*pareirôn*) the laws of the land and the divine Justice
that binds men's oaths, high is his city. No city has he
who in his daring takes to evil. (365-71)[3]

In matters of human relationships, that is, man's capacity is
terrible as well as wonderful. It may destroy as easily as
create. The very capacity with which man's intelligence gifts
him is a dual capacity that "can lead him to the pinnacle of
culture and also to self-annihilation" depending on his moral
ethos,[4] as that is exhibited in action and measured by a full
standard including "the divine Justice that binds men's oaths."
These ominous undertones are present within the wonders
of the first three strophes to rise and sound their note of fear
and warning more dominantly in the concluding lines.

The relation of this ode to the context in which it appears
is also a multiple relation. In the preceding episode an unknown agent is reported to have buried Polyneices' corpse and
done it without leaving a trace. The Chorus has thought that
no one would brave death in this way (220). Its momentary
suggestion that the gods may have been responsible for the
mysterious deed has been violently rejected by Creon (278-
88). A possibility of political sedition has been raised (289-
314). Thus the subject of human daring and resourcefulness,
together with a caution against breaking the laws, forms a
dramatically appropriate theme for the choral ode at this
point. In the main, the Chorus' role and attitude are those
of a loyal supporter of Creon's authority. It has accepted his
leadership previously, and the concluding lines of the ode
appear to repudiate again the unknown breaker of Creon's
edict (372-5).[5]

There are, however, important elements in the ode which
to a sensitive audience must bear wider reference in the dramatic situation than what the Chorus as an actor seems to
perceive. For example, in the final strophe a correlation of
the "laws of the land" and the "justice of the gods" is offered
as the only way in which man's power and ability can be

directed to the good life for the individual and the state. It is apparent that this expression of a joined standard of law and justice offers a fusion of the divergent emphases represented by Antigone in the prologue and by Creon in the first episode. Creon has, to be sure, asserted divine sanction of his edict as certain (282-9; also 184ff., 304-5). But the ode reminds us that the problem is not such as to be resolved by simple assertion, for Antigone has claimed a holy duty (74-7) to which Creon's edict bears no correlation. And in the verses which immediately follow this ode the Chorus expressly terms Antigone's deed as disobedience against "the laws of the king" (382) to suggest further that Creon's law for the land may be only one side of the requisite joined standard. The following episode develops this implication as Antigone and Creon are shown irreconcilably posed on opposite sides in defense of the justice of the gods and the laws of the land, as they each understand them.[6]

Other factors in the ode, as we have previously observed, form suggestive opposing responses to views previously stressed by Creon. Thus with the animal imagery we have observed how the extensive treatment of man's prowess in subduing inanimate nature and the beasts of the earth, including specifically the yoking of cattle and horses, contrasts to the description of man's control of himself and his fellows in the last two strophes. Human control is self-taught, learned rather than imposed (354-6), and it is shown to be a fundamentally different and more difficult attainment because men have a basic moral freedom (365-71). The contrast between the last two and the first two strophes in these terms has a definite bearing for the play as a whole, and this is heightened by Creon's preceding image of yoked draft animals for the citizens of his state (289-92). The evaluative response is reinforced by another of the same sort. Just prior to this ode Creon has made an extended tirade on money as the teacher and director of human conduct (295-312). As the ode here presents the many excellent things man has accomplished with his intelligence, including particularly *"teaching himself such dispositions as regulate cities,"* we are, as it were, offered a broadening correction of view in which to weigh Creon's. And in the final analysis the ode's basic conception of human evil as rooted in man's very wonderful capability is of a much deeper order than the simplifying point of view expressed in his images of the yoke and money just prior to it.[7]

It is possible to find some dramatic "motivation" in the Chorus' attitude for the elements in the ode which question attitudes and policies enunciated by Creon. Many have detected an underlying note of misgiving in the very first words of the Chorus to Creon, as it replies to his proclamation of the edict:

> Such is your *pleasure*, Creon. . . . You have the *means* to use any and every sort of law, both regards the dead and for all of us who live. (211-14)[8]

This in itself should warn us against viewing the ode as a simple extended piece of general moralization working only to support Creon's views. However, the responsions and elements of wider reference which the ode contains are probably not to be regarded strictly as criticisms of Creon's policy by his council of Theban elders. The evaluative suggestions are offered indirectly rather than by direct statement. They arise partly from overtones established in the language, and they are largely a matter of tone and final attitude rather than of dramatic argument. But these internal factors which the poet has established in the ode open a larger range of perception for understanding and evaluating the action. In doing so they fit with the central conception of the ode which we have seen to be a dual or paradoxical conception, and they are not without a certain amount of dramatic preparation in the Chorus' earlier more obvious misgivings about Creon's edict.

## Stasimon II (582-625)

Contrasts of light and dark are prominent in this ode and serve to color, connect, and emphasize elements of the thought. The general view has accepted the ode as an expansive reflection on the divinely cursed destiny of the house of Labdacus and the overall power of fate. As such, it arises naturally out

of the dramatic situation. The Chorus' closeness to the
house (e.g. 164-9) and the sentence of doom just fastened
upon Antigone and Ismene promote such general moralization. This much is obvious and incontestable, as least in terms
of the first two strophes. But it does not take into much
account the stress on human *hyperbasia* (transgression, sin)
or the radiant treatment of Zeus's rule in the third strophe.
And even Jebb, who presses the single fatalistic notion very
strongly, observes a more extensive ominous quality in the
ode reaching beyond the destiny of the sisters and their
family.[9] It may be that attention to some of the sensuous elements of the language by which the poet has expressed his
views can carry us to a closer understanding. Recurrent among
these elements are terms of light and dark more consistently
worked and more pervasive in effect than in any other part of
the play.

Strophe *a* (A)

Fortunate are men who have never tasted of evil:   582
Where once a house has been shaken by the gods,
there Calamity (*atê*) works to the full, creeping on
(*herpon*) from generation to generation:—Just   585
as when a crested wave driven by the savage sea
winds of Thrace runs over the nether darkness
of the sea (*erebos hyphalon*), rolling up black sand
(*kelainan thina*) from the depths, and a low roar   590
sounds from the wind-vexed headlands as they meet
the onslaught.   592

Antistrophe *a* (B)

From times long past I see misery has piled upon
misery and death in the house of Labdacus. Genera-   595
tion frees not generation. Some god dashes them
down and there is no release. So just now over the
last root of the house of Oedipus light was spread;[10]   600
but it, too, now is covered over by the bloody dust
(*phoinia . . . konis*) of the nether gods,[11] by folly of
word and dark fury (*erinys*) of mind.   603

Strophe *b* (C)

O Zeus, what mortal transgression (*hyperbasia*)

57

can restrain your power, that rule that neither all- 605-6
aging[12] sleep can conquer nor the untiring months
of the gods? Ruler in ageless time you hold the
gleaming splendor (*marmaroessan aiglan*) of
Olympus. Through the future and distant time to 610
come, as through the past, this law will prevail,
working not without calamity (*ektos atas*) for the
lives of men throughout this citied world.[13] 614

Antistrophe *b* (D)
For surely far-roving hope is to many men a 616
comfort and to many the deceit of airy desires.
Disillusionment comes to one who knows not until
he burns his foot in the hot fire.—Yes, wise is that
famous ancient saying: evil seems good soon or 620
late to him whose mind god leads to blindness
(*atê*). Only a jot of time does he fare free of ruin
(*atê*). 625

The pattern of lumniference is roughly: major dark (A,
584-94), minor light (B, 599-600), minor dark (B, 601-3),
major light (C, 604-10), and minor light (D, 619), minor
dark (D, 621-5). In sensuous terms there is a strong antithesis
between the first and third strophes, with the second strophe
(B) forming a transition and the last strophe balancing B
to close the whole pattern. This sensuous, imagistic organization is, I believe, supporting of, and sustained within, the
development of "ideas" in the ode; so that we progress from
a deeply fatalistic view centered on the house of the Labdacidae in strophe A to a more extensive and purposive view of
the godhead and of the problem of evil in strophe C. In the
intermediate strophe something of both views is present,
as considerations of human responsibilty and feelings of
superhuman violence are both evoked by the particular situation of the sisters at this time. In the final strophe these same
feelings are caught up and directed to describe the general
plight of men in a universe in which they are responsible
for their conduct but which lies partly beyond their understanding.

We need now to examine the organization of the ode on these two levels of image and idea, strophe by strophe.

(A) In the first strophe the major image of the sea storm portraying the action of the gods upon a house which they have cursed forms a deeply somber and powerful opening. The darkness of the picture even extends beyond the several explicit terms of coloration. At sea, skies are also overcast when the sea shows a "nether darkness," and the gloom beneath the surges is likely to be made the more deep and ominous because of white wave-crests.[14] In the simile the black sand whirled up from the sea bottom adds a further unusual element (590-1),[15] and in the introductory lines before the simile there may also be felt connotations of gloom, both sensuous and emotional. The house is subject to *atê*, not only "calamity" or "ruin," though these seem here major denotations, but already bringing into the ode the suggestion of "blindness" or "infatuation" and probably also bringing at least a memory of the Homeric goddess who blinds men.[16] And it is described as *herpon*, "creeping," "moving slowly," "proceeding darkly." Out of context these connotations would be slight; followed by the deep and extended darkness of the simile, *atê* and its action in this strophe bear an unmistakable somberness and violence.

(C) The third strophe, on the other hand, presents the power and control of Zeus in direct and indirect terms of light, except for the last word which again is *atê*. The quality of light and radiance is not only projected by the strong reiteration in *marmaroessan aiglan* ("gleaming gleam," 610) but may be felt to be extended through Zeus's freedom from Sleep (the son of Night) and from age. This sensuous contrast to the first strophe is paralleled by, and I believe helps to mark, a shift in thought from helpless human suffering under a fateful curse in the first strophe. Here we have not simple suffering but transgression (*hyperbasia*) of men against Zeus's rule and law bringing punishment, and here the godhead is radiant, clear, tranquil and, we may feel, purposeful, as against the tumultuous, dark, imponderable violence of the first strophe. The explicit introduction of *hyperbasia* as transgression and sin with relation to the rule of Zeus, has a particular further significance because of the preceding clash of Creon and Antigone in terms of this word and the divergent canons of duty for which they each applied it (449, 453-5, 481). Thus the theme of transgression has here a double kind of emphasis, from the imagery of the ode and the imagery of the play.[17] And in the final lines a way is suggested by which the apparently antithetical aspects of the godhead, as viewed in these two strophes, are brought together and made mutually supporting. The eternal (radiant) power of Zeus punishes and will always punish transgression wherever met, using as its agent or means (dark) *atê* (611-14). The darkness and violence of the last concept, established in the first strophe, is thus presented as an element of a higher, more judicial and more complex moral order than simply that of a dark, unseeing fate breaking down a family.

(B) The full form and effect of the ode are of course much more complex than this analytical paraphrase. In the ode the action of the gods is not presented as only *seeming* dark and violent; the working out of their control on human lives *is* vividly dark and violent. The first antistrophe (B) as well as the first strophe develops this fact, especially for Antigone. Moreover, the working out of Zeus's law here appears to involve the drastic method of imposing further darkness upon those who in the darkness of self-delusion transgress, until in the end they work their own destruction— i.e. *atê* as infatuation and moral blindness imposed by the gods.

The aural imagery carrying over the dark violence of the storm simile in the opening lines has already been noted (594-8). The last five lines, directed specifically at Antigone, shift the basic image away from the storm but again draw on effects of light and dark (599-603). Specifically the light here refers to the hope vested in Antigone and Ismene for the propagation and continuation of the family. The bloody dust (*phoinia . . . konis*) alludes clearly to the deed which brought them into danger, the dust which Antigone cast on Polyneices' body. The Chorus seems to regard this as an act of thoughtless bravado, and to some of the audience the breaking of social conventions would make Antigone's deed seem furious folly, irrespective of the religious tradition in support of her act. But there are here, too, further suggestions in the language. The final lines of the strophe are bound in with the previous description of the god's destructive action not only by the theme of the family but by associations in the imagery. In the rather unusual use of the term *erinys* (properly a Fury, goddess of the underworld) there are latent suggestions of darkness and divine action—almost of something like *atê* in semi-personified form (603).[18] Reinforcing this close association with the preceding strophe, "the bloody dust of the nether gods" (*phoinia theôn tôn nerterôn . . . konis*), which is said to bring Antigone's end, ties back in point of Infernal origin, substance, and perhaps even in color, to "the black sand" (*kelainon thina*) stirred up by the gods' storm from the depths of the sea's "nether darkness" (*erebos hyphalon*) (589-90).[19] And these various associations sustain the suggestion that Antigone is subject to a violent, dark, external influence. There is in these lines, that is, a fusion of two levels of thought: not only the idea of passionate folly and willful error on Antigone's part, but a larger movement of destruction, beyond simple understanding and beyond just her responsibility. Both possibilities are opened.

As the underlying imagery of light and dark assist in relating these lines closely to the preceding strophe, so they provide elements of transition to the imagery and idea of the third strophe where the idea of reprehensible error and the preeminence of the gods are both caught up but where the emphasis is shifted. There in a more total view "fate" is not simply cruel and external to human effort. *Atê* is a punishment and a punisher for transgression against the rule of Zeus, and the development of this more extensive point of view raises for us implications beyond the "curse" on the house of the Labdacidae and beyond Antigone's particular "fury." For in its full context, as we have observed, the third strophe suggests that Antigone, who was concerned about divine laws and their transgression, may be more right than Creon who accused her of folly.

(D) The final strophe then turns back the emphasis to the darkness of ignorance and *atê*. It catches up the notion of *atê* as infatuation or moral blindness which lies within the second strophe, but it more definitely extends the bearing of this conception to include, as a widespread and basic predicament for men, the simple difficulty of recognizing what is right:

> Surely far-roving hope is to many men a comfort and to many the deceit of airy desires. Disillusionment comes to one who knows not until he burns his foot in the hot fire.—Yes, wise is that famous ancient saying: evil seems good soon or late to him whose mind god leads to blindness (*atê*).[20] Only a jot of time does he fare free of ruin (*atê*).

Here, too, man's overstepping (the foot image as a variant of the transgression images) comes directly in contact with the light image, in a particularized continuation of the imagery of the last strophe. Despite the brightness of the fire, as in the radiance of Zeus's rule, man often simply does not know the right until he is exposed by error to punishment and suffering. Evil seems good; good seems bad. A man's vision grows darker and darker until surely, and with the aid of the gods, he works his own ruin and the divine order is reasserted. This is the tragic way of the *Antigone's* universe, and in compressed form the final strophes of this ode virtually epitomize the tragic universe in which the play is cast. Violence and suffering occur, men are often deluded, the eternal order of the gods works darkly and severely in the lives of the characters but nevertheless is a moral order providing the only rays of final hope and value for human endeavor.[21]

The ode as a whole is a unity whose effect is more than the sum of the diverse sensations, associations, and logically divergent views which it contains. It is intensely meaningful because it does not try to oversimplify problems raised by the action but instead brings together their divergent stresses. Strictly logical cohesion is only a partial criterion here, for the ode as a whole is an effort to relate the moral and emotional aspects of a tragic situation in a tragic universe which embraces human suffering and human blindness together with human moral endeavor and some final principle of value. At this point in the play, the negative elements are naturally prominent in the Chorus' mind, and the qualities of darkness and destruction in the universe are stressed by the poet in keeping with the action. Antigone, the last of the much suffering Labdacidae, appears to be hastening her doom by seeming folly. But the positive factors are also present to extend the bearing of the ode beyond this kind of solution. Thus the ode asserts transgression of divine law as a basic cause of human suffering. The course of the action subsequently works out this principle in respect to Creon, even as it works out Antigone's destruction in keeping with the dark violence and sense of tragic waste which the ode also contains. The multiple bearing of the ode is further apparent because in the matter of "transgression" the ode reiterates her defense of the immortal laws against Creon's "overriding," even though in the initial strophes the ode seems to minimize Antigone's personal efforts. In similar manner, although the Chorus appears to regard Antigone as a victim of delusion and senseless folly in the second strophe, the concluding strophe on human blindness leading to destruction applies finally not so much to her as to Creon. This is certain from the larger context: the primary folly and blindness in the play are Creon's, and they cause widespread ruin. Dramatically it is not fully apparent until later, but the limitation of Creon's vision has already been suggested in the play by the initial developments of the dominant image sequences which we have considered and also by additional elements of the expression which we shall consider later. Here the suggestion of Creon's limitation in vision appears perhaps in its darkest form, more as part of the dangerous and persistent blindness of men than as specifically applied to him. And there is here a further level of "blindness" to deepen the tragic gloom of the situation and of the world in which the play takes place; for the Chorus as an actor does not itself appear to realize the full application of its own observations to the specific situation. In so far as it has supported Creon's edict and continues to do so without seeing what Teiresias later makes explicit, the ancient saying applies also to it: "evil seems good, sometimes."

## Stasimon IV (944-987)

This ode has proved tantalizing to many readers, for its relations to the action seem particularly vague and ambiguous. It occurs immediately after Antigone's final exit under guard to her imprisonment and just before the Teiresias scene. On the surface it offers three mythological parallels to Antigone's situation: the cases of Danaë, Lycurgus, and Cleopatra, each of whom presumably suffered imprisonment. The theme or basic idea about which the examples appear to be grouped is the strange, incontestable power of fate (*ha moiridia tis dynasis deina*, 951-2). The concept is stated twice, once in the opening strophe and again at the close (986-7). On this level, however, the comparisons do not seem to fit any consistent pattern. Danaë was innocent and was honored by a god in her imprisonment. Lycurgus apparently was guilty of a great impiety and was destroyed by a god. Cleopatra and her sons, as presented and so far as known, were helpless and guiltless sufferers. In each case the reasons for imprisonment appear to have been entirely different; the outcomes also varied. The only direct points of comparison of each case to Antigone's situation seem to be noble lineage, probable physical imprisonment, and some vague contact with the strange, incontestable power of fate.

This is not sufficient to explain all that the ode conveys, let alone all that it once may have meant. Lycurgus' case, for example, is not really a lesson in fate, and this divergence itself tends to create a kind of general ambiguity and clash of ideas corresponding to the clash and ambiguity of moral issues raised by the action. The bivalence of attitude can, I think, be shown to be not merely vague and obscurant but rather a constructive, precise compression of different levels

64

of meaning and judgment raised by the actions of Creon and Antigone. Even at the level of general broad effect, the vagueness and divergence of the examples in respect to the stated theme may have a strong normative emotional effect—for example, the effect recorded by Untersteiner, "To what mystery and to what contradiction does Antigone succumb!"[22]

There are, however, at least suggestions that the ode bears much more intimate references to the immediate dramatic situation and to the total context of the play. One cannot pretend to catch with any certainty all its half-hidden allusions and implications for we lack exact knowledge of what may have been the important details of the three myths for the fifth century B.C. audience.[23] Yet, to consider closely what the ode says, including the form the expression takes, and to consider this in relation to the larger context of the play, both reveals several important latent facets of meaning within the ode and provides clues as to what elements of the existing legendary traditions are applicable for its further interpretation. In this way it can be shown that the underlying implications of the first strophe are favorable to Antigone but ominous for Creon; that the deeds and punishment of Lycurgus as described in the ode have strong connotations turning back against Creon beneath an only surface parallel to Antigone; and that the final strophic syzygy carries out this poetic ambiguity, but does so in a manner more intentionally noncommittal from the standpoint of the Chorus' dramatic attitude and role.

But first let us examine briefly two other interpretations of the ode which, on somewhat different, more strictly dramatic grounds, have endeavored to get below the surface of the theme and elucidate some of the inner complexities. First, Ignatius Errandonea seeks to show that the ode is a foreshadowing of the three deaths which are to come.[24] Danaë represents Antigone, the Lycurgus reference suggests Haimon's death, and Cleopatra forebodes Eurydice's suicide. For the second strophe he points out that in several other accounts of the Lycurgus myth Lycurgus killed his own son, Dryas, while trying to stamp out the Dionysiac religion, as in this play it is Creon who in opposing claims of religion drives his son to suicide. The Chorus, Errandonea suggests, foresees what Haimon may do since it has heard him hint self-destruction (751), recognized his dangerous emotional state (766-7), and been concerned with the destructive power of love as it seems to affect him (Stasimon III). The relationship between these aspects of the myth and the plot can, I believe, be supported by further elements in the verbal expression of the strophe. However, in the case of Danaë and Cleopatra it is by no means certain that the legendary tradition pointed to death; in fact, for Danaë the outcome of her imprisonment was special glory and finally even revenge. Furthermore, the connection of Cleopatra with Eurydice can be based only on the fact that Creon's wife lost two sons and came to hate her husband. But the story of only one son is material to this play,[25] and Eurydice's appearance is so far removed in the dramatic action that conscious foreboding in this direction by the Chorus seems unlikely. Finally, therefore, this interpretation seems to insist too much on too close a dramatic working out of the ode, carrying it to a point-for-point relationship between active forebodings, by the Chorus, of events later shown to occur in the same order. Such exact correspondence in terms of character and action alone cannot be adequately supported.[26]

The other interpretation is that of C. M. Bowra.[27] His analysis suggests that the meaning of the ode in terms of the Chorus' attitude is more complex, a matter of conflicting feelings which by alternate expression open wider ranges of emotional and normative response from the audience. As he puts it, "The three stories seem to suggest different interpretations of what is happening and to hint that any one of them may be right." Thus the reference to Danaë may make us feel that Antigone's imprisonment is part of a divine plan to glorify her. But Lycurgus' imprisonment seems a light punishment for one who has insulted god, and the reference to him may suggest that Antigone has been proud to the verge of madness and might have been punished more severely. Cleopatra seems to be an example of great and undeserved suffering and so in conclusion may suggest that Creon's act is wanton brutality. In Bowra's opinion the Chorus has begun to waver and cannot make up its mind, but, because it has started to weaken here, is more ready to accept the message of the god when it comes. Although this interpretation does not try to explain the ode in detail and may be felt to be particularly inadequate for the second strophe, it represents an attempt to accept and explain the multiple implications of the ode, and as such it offers some support to the kind of interpretation which I have outlined. At the same time, there is again in Bowra's interpretation a dramatic pre-occupation which excessively limits the ode. For example, Bowra points only to the conscious attitude of the Chorus as characters viewing the plot action, without regard to the possibility of connotative levels of meaning arising from the mode of poetic expression and perhaps more an intent of the poet than of any specific characters. Secondly, in stressing the wavering of the Chorus' mind as the new dramatic fact which emerges from the ode, as though to give the ode its significance in the tragedy, this interpretation is also open to objection. As will be shown more fully, the Chorus has already displayed an ambiguous attitude toward Creon's justice, particularly during the preceding episode. As an established fact, the wavering of the Chorus' mind alone scarcely merits such major emphasis as would seem to be the case if it were the prime consideration for which the ode is the vehicle.

For our starting point into the detail of the ode we may take an element of the verbal structure—specifically, the emphatic recurrence of yoking images in the first two strophes:

Strophe *a*

Even Danaë in all her beauty endured loss of sun- 944
light in a brazen cell. Hidden in a tomblike chamber
she was *bent to the yoke*. And yet, she was honored 947
in birth—O, child—and she treasured the seed of 950
Zeus, the golden rain.—Yes mysterious and dread is
the power of fate; neither wealth, nor War, nor city-
wall nor sea-beaten black ships can escape it. 954

Antistrophe *a*

He too *was brought under the yoke*, Dryas' son, the
swiftly angered king of the Edonians, when for his
raging taunts he was encased by Dionysus in rocky
bondage. Thus the terrible, exuberant force of his    958
madness seeped away.[28] He indeed came at last to
know the god whom in his madness he had assailed
with taunting tongue; for he tried to stop the inspired    962
maidens and their torch-processions, and he roused to
anger the Muses who love the flute.    965

The two yoking images bracket the general expression of
fate's power so as to draw upon the common conception of
the yoke of necessity, but the recurrence is signally emphatic,
with the second occurrence placed as the lead word of its
strophe. The repetition is vibrant, and within it there is a
level of contrast paralleling and supporting the distinction
that is contained within the other animal images of the play—
the distinction between the question of men harnessing other
men and the role of the gods as drivers of men. The ground
for this distinction has been laid both in Creon's preceding
use of animal imagery and in the first two odes. In these two
strophes the nature of the contrast is reinforced by the clear
shift of emphasis in the antistrophe from the ostensible theme
of general fate to an instance where violence and impiety
are in the forefront. Together these values of the imagery,
in union with the modification of theme, suggest that below
the surface the subject has largely shifted, not only from
Danaë to Lycurgus, but from Antigone as a sufferer to
Creon's action as possibly presumptuous in religious terms.

There are other aspects of these two strophes which point
up the basic contrast lying under the superficial relationship
between the yoking of Danaë, the yoke of necessity, and the
yoking of Lycurgus. In the first strophe the image of yoking
is applied to the action which put Danaë into the brazen
chamber before the action of Zeus is explicitly introduced.[29]
This is in keeping with what is known of the legend's main
outlines. Danaë was imprisoned (bent to the yoke) by her

father, Acrisius, because an oracle foretold that he would die at the hands of his grandson. While in prison she was visited by Zeus. The miraculous union, besides bringing her glory, was the cause of her release, and finally, through the son, Perseus, it proved a means of chastisement to her human yoker, Acrisius.[30] All these developments are not recounted in clear detail in the first strophe, but they are suggested there. Not only is the primary reference of the yoking image to Danaë's imprisonment and sufferings; the glory which she received from Zeus, after and despite imprisonment, is developed into a strong sympathetic affirmation. It is carried not only by a reference to the golden rain but by the phrases γενεᾷ τίμιος (honored in birth, 948) and ταμιεύεσκε (to be a treasurer, 950). The latter term, in its concrete sense fitting particularly well with her golden insemination, connotes also the extreme preciousness of her charge. And this connotation is reinforced by the double reference in the former phrase, "honored in birth"—that is, not only "honored because of her famous descent" but also "honored in and because of her offspring." The opening lines of the strophe refer particularly closely to Antigone.[31] But the concluding lines, stating apparently four symbols of human power which must yield before fate, may be felt to apply much more closely to her human yoker, Acrisius, than to Danaë.[32] He was the king of Argos, with its wealth and power and defenses at his disposal; yet he lost all and was killed by his grandson, Perseus, as the oracle had foretold. Danaë is introduced as more or less helpless, and she would have neither wealth nor military power in her own right, any more than has Antigone. Particularly did Danaë lack powerful black ships. In fact, for us now, because of Simonides' poem and quite possibly for the same reason in the fifth century, Danaë's story is inextricably linked with the small chest in which she and her son were exposed to the sea. To put it most simply, then, in terms of the convenient yoke images, the case of Danaë is in many respects that of a person who is yoked by another human being, without lasting success and with underlying suggestions of final calamity for the yoker.

In the antistrophe, on the other hand, Lycurgus is explicitly and emphatically yoked and subdued by a god as punishment for impiety against the god. This is the major fact which emerges. His case is not really representative of compelling fate, but of sin and punishment, and in this respect it is noteworthy that in his case alone *moira* is not mentioned. His role as a parallel for Antigone herself is suggested only by two rather superficial aspects: he is said to have been "yoked" and to have been encased in some sort of "rocky bondage" (958). This last phrase may be entirely figurative,[33] but in any case the important factors of the agent who applies the "yoke" and of the reasons for the yoking are quite different. The very shift of emphasis to impiety and divine anger would seem basically to disassociate Lycurgus' acts from Antigone's, for not even Creon charges her with impiety.[34] Some of the other references in the strophe are less clear, but they also offer suggestions which cumulatively show the Lycurgus-parallel to point warnings for Creon. The stress upon Lycurgus' madness is striking. Imprisonment alone is a minimum punishment for Lycurgus, but in the other accounts of his career it seems to be the least of the punishments accorded him.[35] In the extant accounts which include the story of his being maddened by the god it is also reported that he killed his son while mad. While, then, it must be conjectural, it is not unreasonable to suppose, as does Errandonea, that these two actions were related in Sophocles' time. In addition to the support for this view which may be drawn from the previous hints of Haimon's suicide, the particularly strong emphasis upon Lycurgus' *mania* in the strophe seems to point to this connection.[36] Not only is the word repeated twice in close succession but the presentation of his madness occupies one quarter of the short strophe given to Lycurgus. To put it another way, if the killing of young Dryas was so tied to the madness story as to be a recognizable allusion, it would at least explain this great emphasis upon an aspect of Lycurgus' actions not otherwise in close relation with our play. If not, we have seemingly purposeless emphasis not in accord with the way in which we have seen the poet work with words. Furthermore, it is probably not mere coincidence that Lycurgus' crime is against "inspired women," for Antigone has been presented as dedicated to the gods, although her gods are elsewhere said to be the nether powers rather than specifically Dionysus.[37] In development of this, as it were, the conflict between Lycurgus and Dionysus is further pointed as a parallel for Creon when in the next ode (Stasimon v) it is Dionysus with his Thyads who is invoked by the Chorus to cure the city of the malady caused by Creon's impiety.

The final strophe and antistrophe devoted to Cleopatra and her sons are even less explicit in their connections to the play, except in the concluding lines. It is not even certain that Cleopatra was imprisoned although it appears so in a late account.[38] According to some of the late versions her sons were half-buried in earth by Phineus after they were blinded, and this may form one element of connection to Antigone's situation which is not generally recognized in the standard commentaries.[39] But in any case the lot of both Cleopatra and her sons is so presented that they figure as more or less helpless victims of great cruelty. In the ode their role as pathetic victims is concentrated in the account of the blinding of the sons and the two lines which form the transition to Cleopatra herself:

... [There Ares] saw the cursed blinding wound struck against Phineus' two sons by his savage wife, darkening the vengeful orbits of their eyes, struck by her bloody hands and shuttle-dagger. (971-6)

Two points in these lines draw attention. Besides picturing the savagery of the agent, Eidothea, Phineus' second wife, the description puts a tight stress on the *blinding* effect. This emphasis is not simply in the repetition of the idea but is also in the strained, compressed use of the two adjectives, *typhlôthen* and *alaon*, which are required to be unusually transitive and vital in their meaning.[40] Then, too, the "vengeful eyes" as here expressed, *alastoroisin . . . kyklois*, are action-fraught, for the primary sense of *alastôr* is of an avenger, one who works vengeance.[41] What is known of the legend accords at least in part with this suggestion. According to all accounts Phineus was blinded by the gods. The reasons given for his blinding vary, but coming together, the emphatic stress in these lines on blinding and the suggestion of vengeance achieved by his sons, both tend to indicate that Sophocles is alluding to Phineus' blindness as punishment for acts of wanton cruelty against the sons of his first wife.[42]

If these veiled suggestions in the strained and pregnant use of the language are accepted, the story of Cleopatra's sons becomes further warning turning against Creon. To be sure, the suggestions lie in overtones, and the final strophe appears to pass over into a simple safe generalization: fate subdued even such a person as Cleopatra, daughter of the wind god.[43] This conclusion is offered as a lesson for Antigone. But it ties the ode into the play at another level, that of the Chorus' dramatic personality as Creon's politically conservative and obedient council. Dramatically the Chorus is not in position to oppose Creon directly, without a major unexplained change in its character, although prior to the ode, as well as in it, there have been definite indications that it questions the rightness of his course.

In summary, then, the ode involves a basic and major ambiguity of meaning and of judgment. The main body of the ode, beyond the simple surface generalization of the power of inexorable fate, involves details which are ominous for Creon and sympathetic for Antigone. This extends even to the point of suggesting eventual glory for Antigone and of recurrently suggesting responsibility and eventual punishment for agents, such as Creon, who seek to subdue others without regard to human rights and higher divine agencies. One cannot be certain of the degree to which the Chorus as an actor is conscious of its own ambiguity in criticizing Creon even as it seems to be dooming Antigone to the strange unfeeling power of fate. One may prefer to see the poet's control more directly at work, so that the ode offers insights and complex workings-out of conflicting levels of judgment beyond the range of the Chorus' rather timorous conscience as the king's council.

In either case there has been preparation in the drama for the different levels of judgment offered by the ode and even preparation for their compression within individual expressions. In the lyric kommos before Antigone's imprisonment the Chorus several times voices sympathy for her in direct terms (e.g. 800-5, 817-19, 836-8). At the same time it is unwilling to support her actively against Creon, and feels uneasy about her self-assurance and her passionate determination (821, 875, 929-30). But despite these reservations there are definite indications in its language, more than once, that Antigone is to be regarded as right and not simply as pathetic.[44] This is a strong implication in 872-5, where the conflict between Antigone and Creon is expressed in reiterated terms of piety juxtaposed to reiterated terms of power as force, even while the Chorus seems to be trying to justify Creon's case. Here the Chorus is addressing Antigone:

> A reverence is due to reverent action (*sebein*); but the man who has power (*kratos*) can permit no overstepping of his power. A self-assured (*autognôtos*) disposition has destroyed you.[45]

And in the last line, even as the Chorus feels uneasy about Antigone's self-assurance, the word used, *auto-gnôtos*, in itself sounds again the conflict between an autocratic ethic (e.g. Creon's power) and the religio-moral tradition represented in the maxim of the Delphic oracle, "Know thyself" (*gnôthi se-auton*).[46] The same affirmative connotation is active when the Chorus calls Antigone "glorious and praiseworthy" (817), and it extends, I believe, into what is one of the key images of the scene, 853-6. The text is debatable, but, with a minimal alteration of the oldest manuscript, the Chorus here says to Antigone:

> Having advanced to the utmost limit of daring you have fallen [suppliant], my child, on the lofty throne of Justice; but you pay out a heavy reward inherited from your father.[47]

In these lines, that is, the Chorus seems to recognize Antigone's claim to a more ultimate, divine order of justice but at the same time to justify her current chastisement on the basis of the family "curse." As such, this evaluation of her fate forms only an indirect and equivocal excuse for Creon's justice, rather than the single strong condemnation of her rashness which is sometimes read into the lines by emending them more radically. And these sympathetic, affirmatory connotations must remain as vital overtones appropriate to the larger context, even if one feels also, as one should, the undertones of criticism in the multiple values of the terms *thrasos* (boldness) and *prospiptô* (fall upon).[48]

All through this kommos between Antigone and the Chorus, then, the Chorus' expression has shades of ambiguity, not only of sympathy for her plight coupled with its own conservative political role, but also with respect to the justice of Antigone's course and the justice that is Creon's. On the one hand, this creates a dramatic wavering of attitude and a degree of final indecision on the part of the Chorus which increases the demands of the action on our pity and fear. On the other hand, it is a poetic means by which the poet makes us aware of the tangled and paradoxical elements of conflict involved in the fundamental moral problems that he has taken as his subject. It is more than just a question of the Chorus' character or dramatic attitude. The broadened, multivalent awareness which is demanded of us here is then directed under skillful control into the Fourth Stasimon where the several emotional and moral meanings of the situation find final intense expression immediately preceding the unmasking of Creon's error by Teiresias.

# CHAPTER V · "AND AT LAST TEACH WISDOM"

~~~~~~~~~~~~~~~~~~~~~~~~~~~~~~~~~~~~~~~~~

Only to the gods does it come never to grow old nor ever die.

(*Oed.Col.*, 607-8)

~~~~~~~~~~~~~~~~~~~~~~~~~~~~~~~~~~~~~~~~~

I N BROAD OUTLINE the conflict of Creon and Antigone embodies diverse ways of looking at reality to find man's place in it and the standards which it may afford for human conduct. Creon on the one hand, we have observed, has a definitely materialistic focus on human motivation, an admiration for a simple, tangible sort of order and considerable confidence in his ability to impose it, and this leads him both to extremes of autocratic conduct (in the social perspective) and to personal catastrophes which require a reorientation of his mode of judging human nature. In the end his eyes are opened to more deep-set principles of morality in life and in the universe. Antigone on the other hand is directly committed to human values of kinship and to a personal and traditional piety that from the first turns to the gods as the final moral forces of the entire system of things which are. In Antigone we see embodied a kind of interior motivation which cannot be measured by the simpler, practical, common-sense approach. Her way is emotional and intuitive, and it leads to her death; yet, in the end the forces of moral decision in the tragedy speak for her: Haimon with the political judgment, Teiresias with his supernatural machinery, and then the catastrophe itself, constructed as it is to underline Creon's error. The placing of the dramatic conflict within the question of man's place in the universe and within the existence of a final tragic order of things we have seen to be accomplished by various features in the imagery, especially in the animal, disease, and sea sequences which run through the play, while at the same time these and the other recurrent

75

images work to develop the motives and attitudes which mark the chief agents of the plot.

Other significant divergences in the modes of expression and the kinds of imagery employed by Antigone and Creon further characterize, and distinguish, fundamentally different ways of looking at reality for normative purposes.[1] They afford us, indeed, further indications of the essential nature of the conflict between these two characters. Along with three additional word patterns that accompany them, they reveal again the close, dynamic interrelationship between imagery, character, action, and theme which constitutes the *Antigone* as a genuine and significant poetic drama.

### *Antigone and the Way of Innate Intuition*

Outside the odes most of the dominant images are used by Creon or are very closely related to attitudes displayed by him. Therefore he has tended to be the focus of the study of the image sequences, and to some degree with disproportionate emphasis. Antigone employs remarkably few images which utilize as their vehicles sensuously concrete and stable referents.[2] Whereas Creon's metaphors consistently employ sensory phenomena and so have an immediate aura of measurable fact, Antigone draws heavily upon direct terms of emotion, and many of her expressions are half-way between imagery and direct emotionalism—for example, her frequent invocations of family allegiances (e.g., 1, 38, 466-7, 857ff., 892ff.) and her recurrent use of such elementary terms of feeling as pain, pleasure, tears, etc., in expressions which we shall consider.

Antigone is, in fact, marked by a strong tendency to think emotionally and feel her judgments as likes and dislikes, love and hate, pleasure and displeasure. For example, in the prologue when opposed by Ismene, she rejects further aid from her sister as "unpleasing" (69-70) and proclaims the rightness of her own course in reiterated terms of love and pleasure: *philê . . . philou meta . . . areskein* (73-4). Shortly after, she again puts her case as giving pleasure where pleasure is due (*areskousa . . . hadein*, 89) and then speaks twice of

hatred for Ismene, hatred from herself and from the dead
(93-4). Expression in emotional black and whites continues
as long as she is in the play. Near the end of her speech on
the unwritten laws, she explains her action in behalf of
Polyneices, three times in rapid succession, in terms of the
pain she would have felt if she had not done the deed (466-8).
In the same episode she describes the opposition between herself and Creon as fundamental, based on what is pleasant
and unpleasant to each of them:

> Why then do you delay? To me nothing that you say
> brings pleasure and it never shall please. And so my
> words are naturally unpleasing to you. (499-501)[3]

And a few lines later she sums up her nature in a finely bal-
anced line:

> It is not my nature to join in hating but in loving.
> (523)[4]

In the kommos preceding her last exit her grief finds partial
expression in somewhat more substantive references (last
journey, last view of the sun, bridal songs, etc.) but her language and attitude throughout are effusively emotional.[5] And
finally her last major speech in the play begins with recurrent
stress on her affection for her family whom she comes to
join (philê . . . prosphilês . . . philê, 898-9), in a further
responsion to lines 73-6 of the prologue.

In addition a strongly emotional and somewhat illogical
method of argument marks her two terminal statements of
final principle, and it is surely above accident that this occurs
thus in her first and her final appearances in the play. Her
first claim of piety for her intended course takes this form:

> I shall bury him. There is an element of beauty to my
> mind to die in doing this. I shall rest loved by him as
> he is loved by me, a "criminal" for holy ends. For it is a
> much longer while that I must please the dead than those
> alive; with the dead I shall rest forever.—But if it seems
> good to you, be guilty of dishonoring the sacred laws
> (ta entima) of the gods. (72-7)

77

Beginning with a strong direct statement of affection, the argument includes a large metaphor. For her the obligation to bury Polyneices seems just as great as the time after death may be long, and in her mind both the obligation and time after death appear to have religious reality. At the same time the form and manner of the metaphor reflect a notable unconcern with the normal processes of logic. For something is strange in the reasoning when *duration* of time to be spent in the underworld proves the value of an act or may be thought to demonstrate its relation to the laws of the gods. This, of course, is not to say that the speech is absurd, for more than logic is involved, and the emotional structure of the expression makes for such immediate intensity that one certainly does not stop to question Antigone's logic. Yet this initial statement of pious principle finds a significant parallel in the more obvious illogic which marks Antigone's last long speech in the play.[6] There she defends her allegiance to her brother's corpse as above any possible allegiance to husband or child:

> If a husband died, I might get another; or a son by another man if I lost the first. But since both my father and mother are hidden in Hades, no brother can ever grow again for me. By such a "law" indeed I have honored you above and beyond all else, my dear brother, and in this I seem to Creon guilty of error and terrible daring. (909-15)

Most recognize this argument as a crude sophism borrowed from Herodotus.[7] Bowra, however, explains it, and probably more rightly, as an unsophisticated and primitive argument, perhaps derived from folklore or the market place.[8] In either case the argument is no clear rational justification of why she gives primary consideration to a brother already dead. She seems to be seeking a basis in the natural processes of generation and death and at the same time to be suggesting another comparative relation: just as much as it would have been her duty to care first for her brother were he alive (as in the case given by Herodotus), so much has she felt it her duty to labor for him after his death. But in this case the emotion obscures the overlapping argument and the result is rational confusion. Yet here again the very illogic of Antigone's argument in her situation helps to convey the special intensity of her feeling for her brother. For her, her relationship with him is a paramount fact and it demands a special kind of loyalty, the logic of a more pragmatic world to the contrary.

Two major aspects of Antigone's role in the play are emphasized by her directly emotional and sometimes almost extrarational mode of expression. One is a certain separation of her thought from the plane on which most of the other characters move, prior to the peripety. The other is her possession of a kind of immediate moral intuition, which though almost consistently underestimated and misunderstood by those with whom she comes in contact, yet is shown in the end to be a genuine and significant insight. These two facets of her role cannot be fully separated, though the former is perhaps more specifically dramatic and the latter more thematic. They are in great measure parallel and interconnected results of the same emotional tendencies which we observed in her expression.

The separation of Antigone's thought seems sometimes to be a more divisive split than simply from the other characters of the play, for she regularly proves a difficult character for critics to understand closely. The difficulty is in some measure a result of her preference for direct emotional expression. Direct emotion directly expressed is likely to seem either private or blatant in literature, and to some degree the depiction of Antigone is subject to these dangers. If her many statements of judgment drew more often upon concrete external referents, Antigone might very likely appear to be a less private character, one whose attitudes could be more closely shared and sharply defined. There is instead a certain untouchability about her, coupled with a kind of internal vehemence that eludes close sharing. Yet these very qualities which promote misunderstanding are utilized with considerable effectiveness in the play for other purposes than to make her a complete person or an intimately "human" character.

The difficulty in understanding Antigone precisely and warmly is directly related to the fact that no one with whom she comes in contact does seem fully to understand her. Not only in respect to Creon but very largely also in respect to the Chorus and Ismene she moves in her own realm, self-knowing (*autognôtos*) and self-legislating (*autonomos*), separated by her own immediate sense of goal and by the concentration of her determination. Her isolation has often been remarked.[9] It is achieved in various ways and appears most carefully conceived. In individual scenes, as we have observed, a high degree of tension is created by having Antigone and Creon use the same or similar terms to mean radically different things. And because of her isolation from the full understanding and partnership of the other characters, strong tragic irony is achieved for the final portions of the play, when, after the catastrophe cannot be avoided, the major forces of right are explicitly shown to have been with her. This telling dramatic isolation of Antigone is achieved in part precisely through her direct emotional mode of expression. As she dismisses the considerations raised by Ismene and Creon by answering in direct terms of love and hate, pleasure and displeasure, she at once removes herself from the level of their thought and the circle of their understanding. Arguments raised by the other characters come to seem largely external to her, and none of them manages to divert her emotional concentration on what she feels to be her necessary and pious duty. In the kommos prior to her final exit, lack of affection and the sorrows of her family do act upon her and shake her, but these are also forms of her particular internal, feelingful sort of awareness, and they do not turn aside her sense of special direct allegiance to her dead family and brother.

Antigone herself has a close sense of insight, a feeling of knowing, that is vibrant even if not always precise in her expression. She is not isolated to a level of empty passion but to a direct and special sense of intuition which in the end

80

is shown to be finally more accurate, morally and religiously, than the supposed practical wisdom (*phronêsis*) with which Creon is cloaked. Several further facts contribute elements of substance to the emotive and sometimes other than rational quality of Antigone's expression. In part, that is, the strength of tradition is with her in her defense of allegiance to family and of the sanctity of burial, even where enemies are concerned.[10] The rhetoric of her famous speech on the unwritten laws and the final tribunal of the gods (450-70) is not marked by any suggestion of logical inconsistency such as is observable in her first and last statements of final principle. With controlled, sure eloquence it raises, as it were, the powerful voice of religious tradition against Creon's impiety. In so doing it provides essential background for the understanding of his error and the woes that later befall him. But here, too, intense personal feeling is a strong element permeating Antigone's belief and coloring this her central statement of principle. It finds expression both in the emphatic use of the first person and in the reiterated voicing of the *pain* she has avoided by doing what she sees to be her duty (465-8).[11] The immediacy of Antigone's feeling, the directness of her sense of moral duty, is, in fact, what vitalizes this speech so that it not only puts before us the vision of traditional piety but embodies the age-old religio-emotional intuition with an intensity beyond the force of general traditionalism. In other connections, as we shall observe more fully later, there is developed the further suggestion that Antigone's insight and her cause are natural as distinct from what may be only conventional. The distinction, shaded-in by a recurrent interplay between the terms *physis* and *nomos*, contributes an additional underlying sense of substantiality to her particular emotional way. In some measure, that is, Antigone is identified with nature and its abiding surety, and we are to feel this with her when she says,

It is my nature (*ephyn*) to join in loving, not in hating.
(523)

Dramatically Antigone is of course more complicated than a mere type-presentation of human moral emotion and intuition. There is anguish as well as conviction in her final speeches. There is the harshness displayed toward her sister, which some have taken as the key to the *hamartia* that is thought necessary to justify her death by Aristotelian post-scriptions.[12] Her harshness to Ismene not only serves effectively to increase Antigone's dramatic isolation; it brings to attention the danger of such direct moral intuition, even as the speech on the unwritten laws illustrates the heights to which it can reach. But this cruel aspect of Antigone's character is minor and not to be magnified into a "tragic flaw." Antigone's impassioned concentration on what she feels to be the major issue is surely the crucial part of her character, for it impels her to oppose Creon. In the end it is impossible to view her defiance as erroneous or write off its motive impulses. From the start the mainsprings of Antigone's course show themselves in her vocabulary and her mode of argument: direct emotional devotion to her brother and family and, conjointly, a strong belief (feeling) that her action in burying Polyneices is piety. In the end, subsequent to her disappearance from direct view, the course of the tragedy reveals that her sense of direct and true insight in these motives is justified, has been an accurate intuition, according to the standards of the divinely maintained moral order which Teiresias and the form of Creon's chastisement bring into the action of the play as the final basis of right and wrong.

### Creon and the Way of Sense and Reason

Creon bears a much larger part in the *Antigone* than does Antigone herself and is a more sharply and fully delineated character, but he is not therefore necessarily a deeper, more significant one. He is not simply reason in simple opposition to Antigone's emotion, for he, too, is an effective character with human and dramatic complexity, and not just a type. He definitely is not a simple figure of baseness or villainy of intent as contrasted, say, to a purity of motive in her. Creon has a set of ethical principles of a sort, including strands of what he considers to be piety, and he is by no means insincere in his efforts to apply his principles. By and large his concrete and common-sense approach to the problems which face him is for a long time, in contrast to Antigone's emotionalism, in seeming tune with the exigencies of the practical world as most people see it. However, central in the characterization of Creon, or in the problem raised by his character, are clear indications that his perception is limited in depth and that his mode of thought is inadequate to deal with the deeper sources of human motivation and problems of moral value. Thus we have been able to observe how the dominant image sequences characterize Creon's vision as pragmatic, materialistic, and limited in range and how at the same time they set his estimations of human motivation and value in the perspective of a larger more inclusive vision of life. These factors, we have seen, are developed first by implication and then in explicit reiteration. The severity of Creon's kind of limitation is, in fact, strongly intensified because throughout the first three-quarters of the play Creon's mode of thought and his analysis of the situation are presented as the rational, sensible point of view as against Antigone's private intuition and intense emotionalism. And here three additional patterns, partly imagistic and partly ideational, demand particular attention for the manner in which they help to project into the play the conflict between the rational, man-made, and empirical as against the intuitive, permanent, and essential. These are the *phronein* motif and the imagery of sight and the *nomos-physis* pattern.

### PHRONEIN-APHROSYNÊ

A distinctive, recurrent stress on terms of thinking in part sets the problem of knowledge, of different kinds of knowledge and different ways of thinking, as a critical issue for the play. Creon in particular repeatedly presents his views and his policies as "right thinking" (*to phronein* and similar terms), while those who are opposed to him he regards as "irrational" (*anous*, etc.),[13] and these same terms serve until the catastrophe to distinguish his and Antigone's mode of judgment.

83

In the conclusion they give biting, ironic reverse to the sensible, practical reasoning power which Creon has thought was his. This *phronêsis-aphrosynê* motif, as it has been called, starts favorably to Creon, twists sharply against him in the scene of peripety, and is twice sounded in the five lines which conclude the tragedy.[14] Speaker after speaker dwells on the thing he thinks is "rational" or "wise." For nearly a thousand lines all except Haimon attribute "senselessness" or "unreason" to Antigone and regard Creon as the man with mind.[15] But with the Teiresias scene this antithesis is reversed. Teiresias turns the terms against Creon (996, etc.);[16] Creon is then seen as ill-minded, *kakophrôn*, by the Chorus in 1104; to the Messenger Creon's work is a lesson that thoughtlessness, *aboulia*, is the greatest of human ills (1242-3); and finally Creon himself strongly condemns his own mistaken counsel, *dysboulia*, in 1261-9.[17] The Chorus concludes the play with the observation that wisdom, *to phronein*, is the supreme requirement of life but that real wisdom comes late if at all. At the end it is clear that for wisdom one is not to understand merely rational assurance, the main denotation of the various terms of knowledge for the major portion of the play. The wisdom of the conclusion includes a feelingful sense of human obligations and limitations. It includes not only the means of work-a-day success but also a pious reverence for the gods and the instruction which comes through suffering.

### THE IMAGERY OF SIGHT

Closely reinforcing the treatment of knowledge in the abstract is specific imagery of sight given both verbal and dramatic form. The progressive development of this more or less elemental metaphor has also particular bearing in marking the quality and the final limitation of Creon's vision, and, as it does so, it has a cardinal unifying role for the questions of degree of insight and of point of view that are raised in so many forms through different elements of the tragedy. Thus the character of Creon's imagery is consistently sensory and concrete, directed to the eye and touch and practical

experience, as, for example, in his application of the animal
and monetary images and also in such vividly sensuous passages as his observations on marriage (648-54). In the first
part of the play he also tends to stress terms of seeing, and
he specifically dislikes that which is hidden over or obscured
from direct sight. Consider, for example, line 206 ending
*idein*, line 307 with the phrase *es ophthalmous emous*, and in
line 760, *kat' ommat(a)*, where in each case these terms of
concrete visualization are an otherwise pleonastic addition
to the expression.[18] The Haimon scene, which includes the
last example, brings the sight imagery to mounting prominence. Haimon's initial efforts at conciliation recognize his
father's distrust and ignorance of what is hidden from view
and urge his own special ability to bring to light the truth
from out of the dark of public opinion (690-700). Then, at the
close of the scene, just prior to his angry exit, Haimon is
made to reply to his father's visual tautology in an emphatic
reiteration of Creon's terms:

You will never look on my head again to see it with your
eyes. (763-4)

Creon's preference for the linear, measured, and simply ordered also gets emphasis in this scene and is obviously related
to his primary trusting in his own powers of inspection.[19]
Together these attributes of Creon's manner of thought,
which for a long time give his expression the quality of practical grasp and sensible realism, prepare specifically for the
Teiresias scene. For the introduction of the blind seer to
engineer the peripety and effect the recognition is in this play,
as in the *Oedipus Tyrannus*, a masterful dramatization of the
imagery of sight to bind together in a major symbol the
various aspects of the question of vision which have been
raised in play. In the *Antigone* it climaxes the sight imagery
and reveals its meaning conclusively. Just as the old seer
leaning on the boy gives the reverse symbol to Creon's repudi-
ation of his son and the feelingful piety of youth, so also now
the seeing man is blind and the blind man sees. The man of
assured reason is shortsighted; the mystic seer looks through

to the end. The apparent is not real; the real is not always easily apparent when it is human life and human values that are at stake.

It is of course in the *Oedipus Tyrannus* that we get the perfect climax of a mounting sight pattern in the self-blinding of Oedipus. Here Creon's recognition comes earlier, and the manipulation of the sight imagery is at lesser tension. But it is also effectively sustained in the final scene of this play by a further reversal of the imagery which looks almost as though it may have been germinal of the conclusion effected with Oedipus. In the final scene Creon in part wishes a darkening of the physical vision that has misled him (1328-33), and in part he has assumed the posture of the blind seer, leaning on his servants and unable to walk his own way in the world (1320-5, 1339). But it is now that Creon has insight. Now at last he is said to have "*seen* justice" (1270) as he takes on responsibility for the catastrophe.

### NATURE AND LAW

An active concern with justice and law and their relation to reality extends back to the start of Greek literature and is a marked feature of this play, closely bound up with the treatment of practical intelligence and the matter of insight into a final order of values. Interworking terms of *physis* (origin, nature, generation) and *nomos* (custom, law, convention) provide an important additional fix on the basic attitudes toward human value and human motives that are represented in Creon and Antigone. The terms of the three patterns, and especially of this one with that of "reason," are repeatedly juxtaposed, as by Ismene in the prologue:

> But now . . . *see* in what utter misery we shall perish if in violence to law and custom (*nomos*) we pass over a king's decree and powers. No, we must hold in mind (*ennoein*) this fact, that we are women not born (*ephymen*) to war with men. (59-62)

Starting from this point where particular decree, social convention, physical quality and supposed common sense are

86

all grouped as one by Ismene, the poet has exploited the terms to open to us more penetrating questions: What is human nature, what is law, in what sense is law natural and nature lawful, what is the place of human intelligence in defining law and in respect to nature at large? No precise philosophical definitions are offered, and we are not entitled to expect a thoroughly logical solution to the many facets of the *nomos-physis* issue, which by all evidence was just beginning to become one of the critical jousting grounds of professional philosophers at this time.[20] In the way of poetry and of action we are given instead some of the quality of experience as it bears on the central issue of man's relation to the kosmos through nature and law, and we are led experientially to the lines of insight which the poet had developed with respect to it.

Thus Ismene's initial suggestion is that law (*nomos*) is what the ruler sets and that obedience to it is the role of human nature, especially of feminine nature. This view is developed by Creon with valid implications for the good of the community but also with mounting suggestions of the relative nature of *nomos*. In his first speech he urges that a man's judgment and mind can be known only when he is tested in leadership and law-giving (*nomois*) (175-7), and he goes on to subordinate considerations of friendship and kinship to the welfare of the state. These, he says, are his *nomoi*, the principles of rule, behind his edict (192-3). In the generally conventional and altruistic tone of the speech to this point we feel the genuine need of subordinating personal rights to principles found best for the social whole.[21] But when Creon has finished the pronouncement of his edict, the ambiguous reply to the Chorus takes us somewhat further, to seeing possibly less objective grounds beneath Creon's *nomoi*. It is in his power, it says, to use any sort of *nomoi* that please him (211-14). By the second episode, *nomos* is to Creon specifically his own edict (444-9), and when Antigone counters that only Zeus and the goddess *Dikê* can define *nomoi* in such matters, both he and the Chorus see her as one who has simply inherited an excessively stubborn mode of

87

thought (471-4). As the action progresses, Creon becomes recurrently emphatic about the proper—i.e. customary and physiological—subservience of women to men,[22] and in the process he denies the relevance of blood relationship (*ta eggenê physei*, 659), while this matter is of course to Antigone a primary natural fact of greatest moral weight. Thus in the third episode Creon presents to his son a thoroughly pragmatic, naturalistic approach to the family, in which *physis* figures simply as physical generation with its value to be measured by whether one's offspring help one or not (641-60; cf. 569). The dominance of male over female, regarded both physically and sociologically, is here also for Creon a symbol of the rightful power of a leader over the state; that is, law (*nomos*), by naturalistic analogy, is merely a function of power (659-65). The ethical relativism within this point of view is soon after brought to the forefront when Creon and Haimon split openly on whether the city is to get its rights and directions from one man or whether it belongs to the many and must include religiously ordained principles of justice (733-49).[23]

As against the naturalistic and rationalistic attitude which is developed in Creon's use of terms of *nomos* and *physis* prior to the peripety, the view reflected in Antigone's use of the terms is instinct with feelings of more fundamental grounds for law and for values. She finds the valid principles, the *nomoi*, of life both in her own nature and in the religious tradition of "unwritten laws" maintained by guardian spirits of the kosmos. Thus on the one side she holds up Zeus and Dikê and Hades as the definers of the laws of burial and family duty and offers herself to their court as specifically distinct from the reasoned opinions and legal ordinances of men (450-60, 511-23). And at the same time the natural fact of her blood-relation with her family is to her a prime reality, almost a law in itself (511-23).[24] It is out of this fact of family that she draws the line that we have previously quoted:

It is my nature (*ephyn*) to join in loving, not in hating.
(523)

Antigone also feels the weight of incest and suffering in the blood or *physis* of her family as a factor helping to cut her off from more normal objects of love (857-71). This is a dark undertone in the *physis* pattern as it relates to her, as elsewhere the rudimentary elements of conflict which sometimes spawn within natural kinship are recognized by Sophocles.[25] But in the same scene we find Antigone identifying herself with nature in the larger sense as she invokes the springs and groves of Thebes to witness by what sort of *nomoi* ("laws of men") she is being doomed (842-56; cf. 937-43). Here, too, her extended final statement of principle includes at root a claiming of a *nomos* within *physis*, a law pegged in the nature of things as they are for her.[26] As a woman without children she might yet get some; as a woman whose brothers and parents are dead, no natural process can recover her brother to her. Only by such a "law," she says, does she oppose the civil will. At this point the argument carries little weight with the Chorus or Creon. Its manner, we have seen, is such as to draw comments of naïve or crudely sophistic. But the fact of the matter is that after Antigone has left the stage, and only then, we get the measure of the validity which lies in her instinctive identification of *physis* and *nomos* as part of her identification of herself with a final order of things that is partly natural and partly divine.

In the scene of peripety the dependence of genuine "law" upon "nature," their interdependence within a cosmic unity of things, is imaged concretely and extensively in the first part of Teiresias' warning. The normal means of augury by which men through the intermediacy of natural phenomena learn the will of the gods have been thoroughly confounded by the course of events (997-1013). And in this pivotal scene the emphatic imagery of disease has also the effect of binding together the workings of men's minds, the character of the laws, the order of nature, and the finally controlling workings of the gods in nature (e.g. 1015-18). The same fact is written in again with grimly climactic appropriateness as Creon here is told that he shall pay with one "from his own flesh and blood" (*tôn sôn . . . ek splagchnôn*) unless he acts to correct his error.[27] The devaluer of family relations is to learn their innate value by experience if in no other way.

Various features of the pattern up to this point bear on the place and limits of intelligence. The second ode is obviously of particular significance in this connection. The inventive, organizing power of human thought has brought men power over external nature and enabled them to discover also the advantages of "such dispositions as regulate cities" (*astynomous orgas*). But there are limits. Over death men's minds have no control, and the clever facility of human intelligence, we are reminded, involves great dangers for the individual and the state unless men learn "to weave together the laws of the land and the justice of the gods." The same total view is latent in the Haimon scene, though expressed differently. Haimon speaks of man's mind as his greatest inborn or natural gift from the gods (683), and he cautions Creon that men are not usually so constituted as to have entire wisdom (719-23). Creon on the other hand is confident of the superior nature of his thought processes on the basis of superior age (*phronein . . . physis*, 726-7) and feels that his legislation is sufficiently grounded on these two facts. The road which Creon has to take to a more deep-reaching, less self-assured wisdom is a hard one. While he later accepts Teiresias' evidence so far as to recognize that "to keep the established laws is best even to life's end" (1113-14), he finds this out too late. Finally, in the actual loss of his son he learns more intimately both the value of natural kinship and the magnitude of his previous error (1261-9). And significantly here at the end, when Creon has come to realize in terms of his blood-kin his previous ill-reason, the issues of intellect, nature, justice, and insight are brought together to a resolution, for it is at exactly this point that Creon is finally said to have "*seen* justice" (1270).

In the characterization of Creon as we see him through most of the *Antigone* there are distinct traces of the "enlightened," rationalistic attitude identifiable with the Sophists or with the so-called Sophistic movement which came to prominence in the second half of the fifth century B.C.[28] To some extent we get this in the dominant image sequences which mark Creon's thought as materially grounded and pragmatically directed. We may feel it also to some extent in the doctrinary pose and carefully formed argumentation of some of his longer speeches (e.g. 162-210, 639-80), in his efforts to reason away the involvement of divine interest in his affairs (e.g. 280ff., 1040-4), and in his progress under pressure toward a doctrine of power as the norm of conduct (730-61). But the most probing development of these "sophistic" attributes, which also reaches out extensively in its bearing for human conduct and self-estimation, is the striking treatment of the subject of intellection (the *phronein* and sight patterns) as it is coupled with the deployment of terms of "nature" and "law" between Creon and Antigone. Through these means Antigone's emotive and pietistic mode of insight to a final reality is set not only against the strong down-to-earth, inductive quality of thought embodied in Creon's many concrete images, but specifically against a man of "mind" whose focus is naturalistic and whose confidence is in the empirically based reason.

Unfortunately the most graphic and only nearly adequate record of the great figures of the Sophistic advance toward rational, empirical and naturalistic modes of thought comes from over a half century later in the dialogues of Plato. Records more nearly contemporary to the *Antigone* are so scanty that it is impossible to pin-point precisely, in the way history would desire, the particular figures or teachings that may have influenced Sophocles' presentation.[29] It is obvious, however, that "the spirit of devotion" and the traditional bases of morality were under strain by the middle of the fifth century and that Sophocles, like Aeschylus in the *Oresteia*, has taken as part of his mission the reassertion of their validity in the stuff of experience. By 442/1 B.C., that is, expanding geographical horizons, great economic prosperity, the democratical rise of the commercial classes, and the sudden ascendence of Athens to a position of world leadership had led to a reshaping of old institutions and necessitated adaptations of thought and practice for the opportunities of a competitive world of practical realities. At the same time advances in technology, scientific observation, and cosmological speculation, including an increased awareness of the diversity of peoples and of norms of conduct, had extended the sphere of the intellect and brought into question such basic ideas as "god," "nature," "law," and "knowledge."[30] The *Antigone* stands at an early point in this intellectual fermentation of the late fifth century, so far as that proto-Enlightenment is recorded. In the figure of Creon and in its treatment of the powers of the mind, the relation of justice to reality and the matter of the sight and insight, the play seems to foresee and offer a strongly ironic caution against the impending disintegration of tradition before the hand of opportunism and the eye of rational scepticism. It is certain, for instance, that a major battle between final values and the relative nature of institutions was fought out in terms of *nomos* and *physis* during the final four decades of the fifth century with the physical philosophers, such as Democritus, and the Sophists, such as Antiphon, advancing the cause of the relative.[31] This historical conflict of ideas, in fact, provides lines for Plato's reinterpretation of values and of reality whereby he reinserted the human conceptions of law and justice into the very structure of the cosmos.[32] With Plato's reinterpretation, as Jaeger says, "Philosophy returns at the end of its journey to the conception of justice which we [find] at the beginning of Greek history, only at a higher level of consciousness."[33] At the date of the *Antigone*, 442/1 B.C., Sophocles may never have encountered a precisely reasoned and thoroughly conscious expression of the relationship (or the disrelationship) of *nomos* and *physis*. But he was thoroughly alive to the basic issue which the terms embody, the issue of sheerly pragmatic as against values of a more ultimate nature, and in the *Antigone* he offers one of the first known attempts to probe and focus this issue in the specific and telling terms of "nature" and "law." If the mode is experiential and poetic rather than strictly logical, yet it speaks to the consciousness of men, and it was in Greek tragedy at large a genuine force against surrendering the world to the subjectivists—and, so, of keeping the field open for the mobile striking power and heavy artillery of Platonic dialectics.

## The End is Wisdom

It is clear from the play itself, irrespective of outside evidence, that the world presented itself to Sophocles as a scene of radical tension in which manifestations of the intelligence, ability, strength, and even the occasional greatness of men existed for him close beside the reality of evil, uncertainty, presumption, and fear. The second ode (Stasimon 1) gives this deep-set polarity particularly intense expression:

> Wonders are many and none more awesome than man. . . . Ever resourceful mind of man (*periphradês anêr*). . . . Words and wind-swift thought has he fashioned to his use and the dispositions that regulate cities. . . . Possessed of wise contrivance, clever beyond all measure, now to good he moves and now again to evil. . . .

In one form and another we have been able to trace this tension between human accomplishment and weakness, insight and blindness, finality and finiteness as Sophocles has built it into a tight, many-leveled complex of attitudes and issues about the conflict of Creon and Antigone. For the poet it was not enough to reduce experience to the variformed monochrome (valuewise) of naturalism nor yet to be satisfied with the simplifying optimisms of the would-be rational mind. He reacts, we can observe, specifically against each in his treatments of knowledge, law, and nature, and with these he has carefully marshaled imaginative and experiential evidence throughout the tragedy which asks us to feel that there are springs of human motivation and levels of experience which still bind man more deeply into a moral order extending throughout the system of things that are.

In Creon's final speech in the play there is a particularly vibrant reprojection of his tendency to base his judgment on the immediately tangible and obvious:

93

I know not which way to *look*, or where I may *lean*. For whatever my *hands* touch goes *aslant*, and all in all a terrible *heavy* fate has *leaped* down on my *head*. (1341-6)

The successive concretes of elementary perception and especially the image of *lechria* (slanting, oblique, awry), throwing back on Creon's former readiness to judge according to the evidence of his eye and reflecting his admiration for the straight and easily proportioned, give intense and sharp reminder of his earlier disregard for what might lie below the purview of his primary senses. The three lines thus recapitulate his failure to understand, during most of the play, the human and religious realities which lie beyond his reasonable practical view based upon the concrete and obvious. For finally the tragedy of Creon is not that he was evil in intent or even that he aspired to political tyranny but that he was limited in his "rational" and factual wisdom and did not know it until terrible events which he had initiated came down heavily on his own head. To Creon's materialistic rationalism Antigone's innate feeling serves both as a foil, partially illustrating the shortsightedness of such a view as his, and as a corrective, offering a complementary way of knowing. At the same time both the action and the main lines of the verbal structure offer as an important complicating factor the fact that her way of knowing is usually thought less acceptable than Creon's. This aspect of the *Antigone* lies close to the center of the play's meaning as it is embodied not only in the material of these last analyses but also in the whole image structure of the play so far as we have been able to observe it.

The central pervasive place of the problem of knowledge in the *Antigone* is signaled explicitly in the concluding lines spoken by the Chorus. These lines in effect state the theme of the whole in a highly compressed form.

Wisdom (*to phronein*) is much the primary base of happiness, and men must avoid irreverence to the gods. The big words of the proud earn big blows and at long last teach wisdom (*to phronein*). (1347-53)

94

In the play as a whole, as in these lines, the issues are strongly moral and religious as well as intellectual. Questions of value and worth, of motive, authority, and governance, are presented as inseparably bound in with questions of understanding and perceptiveness. The central vision which has informed the tragedy is, it seems, a vision of the limitation of human vision in the face of a world in which there is a deep-set moral meaning that stands as the final stake of all human endeavors. The tragedy is a dramatization of moral blindness and error as they generate misunderstanding and destruction because of failure to recognize the principles of moral order maintained by the gods and also exhibited in certain fundamental human feelings and aspirations for lasting value.

Obviously the content of the play is much more than the final tag by the Chorus or any summary statement of the theme. In simplest terms the dramatic vehicle is the conflict of two persons in respect to a burial. Besides the personal clash, their conflict is made to involve larger issues of various sorts: ethical issues (problems of family allegiance and conflicting views of personal conduct), political issues (systems which permit or encourage each way of life), religious issues (the sanctity of burial, the nature of piety, the attitude of the gods to human conduct) and philosophical issues (the nature of the individual, his means of knowledge, the relation of nature and law, the moral ordering of the universe). These issues are interwoven and interdependent, organized with a logic which springs from the duality of the central vision and presented in the particular, sensory, emotional and many-leveled mode of poetic drama, not in the mode or logic of philosophy.

A vision of limited vision, applied in both its significations: the ease of human illusions and the inner vision of the "blind" — the phrase tightly sums up the theme of the *Antigone*. In this study we have approached it primarily through the elements of expression and character. First with single image sequences, then with the more intricate expression of the odes, and finally in the language and thought of the major agents, we have observed how the diction is organized in its structural significances for the whole. In this ancient Greek play, the relation of the verbal imagery and the theme appears, in fact, to be very like that described by the modern English poet and critic, C. Day Lewis:

"Whether in verse then, or in prose, the principle that organizes images is a concord between the image and the theme, the image lighting the way for the theme and helping to reveal it, step by step, to the writer (or reader), and the theme as it grows controlling more and more the deployment of the images. If verse is still the best medium for the poetic image, it is because the whole mode of verse, by its formal limitations and its repetitiveness, can create a greater intensity within the image patterns—clearer echoes, more complex relationships."[34]

But, actually, situation and action as well as expression and character are all so shaped in the *Antigone* as to project the central vision with a concentrated ironic intensity that organizes a deep range of experience. Our treatment has implied this often and illustrated it in part at various places. If now we return to the initial notion that the plot of agents in action is in a sense the basic image of the whole, we may recognize that what we have in the *Antigone* is an organization of various kinds of analogies: in situation (or scene), in action, in character depiction, and in verbal expression, each in its own mode projecting some aspect or part or implication of the total vision which is the poet's play.[35]

Thus, although the antecedent tradition on the myth is to us now somewhat uncertain, we may observe that the mythical situation or scene in which the play is cast itself is such as to create a series of severe tensions: between traditional burial rights and treasonable aggression, between family ties and civic solidarity, and, perhaps less essentially in the matter of sexes, between the value of an individual person and restrictive social mores. In the mythic background of the scene also the incestuous history of the family of Oedipus recurrently projects lines of doubt across these other issues. The plot, meantime, sets a man in high and respected position of state authority over against a woman of unusually emotional and somewhat one-sided concentration, a self-chosen and vehement protagonist of human and religious values which he does not recognize as bearing upon the particular situation. Instead of a central tragic figure we have, that is, "a double center of gravity" for the action, and this device of plot in itself sets up a strong polar tension even as it extends the bearing of the expression, illustrating the various issues from radically divergent points of view. Through the first half of the play virtually all the obvious forces are disposed to credit the leader's judgment and discredit the woman's breaching of civic order. This tension and the paradoxical turn which the action is to take have an analogy in the cross tension produced as each of the main figures, in the first half of the play, gains support from the one who should naturally be the closest intimate of the other. We refer here, of course, to Ismene in the prologue and to Haimon. These ironies of action find their climactic dramatic analogy in the scene of peripety, in which dramatization of the sight imagery is so marked a feature, and we are here shown explicitly by the blind seer that the basic conflict is taking place at a level where the claims of the seemingly practical and immediate (including what is now sometimes called "realistic" politics) are in direct conflict with a more basic kind of reality. The conclusion avoids trivial oversimplification of this fact. The woman is destroyed partly by her own emotional will, partly by an error of timing on the part of the leader who is now bent on rescue, and partly as a carry-over of the distorted direction of power in the leader's previous efforts to assert his own standards. The leader is reduced to a bitter awareness of his limitations and grave wrongs by a series of deaths which result from his action and which at the same time also reflect unmistakably the reaction of the gods against his breaching of the final moral order that they maintain. The directing vision is consistent in whole and in parts: the difficulty of human knowledge for the valid exercise of moral responsibility and the fact that men are, nonetheless, responsible to standards beyond themselves and may be forced finally to this insight through the exercise of a tragic process which includes suffering and destruction as its basic procedures.

Little more needs to be said on the two protagonists by way of summary. Antigone gives her name to the play probably both because she is the more unusual and daring creation and because she finally most represents the right in the complicated interplay of ends and means which the play presents. This is not to say that her way of emotional piety is considered self-adequate, any more than that Creon's sincere efforts at reasoned understanding and civic stability are offered for simple condemnation. The fact of the two protagonists and the kind of tension which is generated between them is direct testimony to the fact that Sophocles himself here sees life whole and would not have us commit ourselves to just one or another mode of knowing. Generally speaking, with respect to the ends and means of human understanding as they are offered us here, Antigone is perhaps more limited in means than ends and Creon more inadequate in respect to end. Both, that is, are partial in the ways of understanding which most markedly distinguish them, and both are agents of significance. Even after she leaves the stage Antigone is more than a "sufferer." For finally viewed, it is her insight which has been correct, and it is she who is the rallying point of the forces of vision in the crossing issues of personal ethics, politics, philosophy, and religion through which the action moves. But at the same time there can be no doubt that Creon is the more closely developed and dramatically dominant character. Not only does he occupy a larger portion of the stage-time; his errors and punishment form the major concern of the last third of the play and are the most obvious unifying strand of the double plot. As he stands at the end externally broken, internally humbled, and at last fully conscious of the depth of his responsibility, it is, moreover, Creon who draws most fully on our sympathy and who comes closest to embodying in himself a full attitude toward the tragic world we have seen unfolded. That this is so and that this seems so inevitably the "necessary" conclusion for the tragedy is in great measure the product of the logic of ironic progression which has been made to carry through all aspects of the structure. In the wreck of Creon's world and his new consciousness of the heart, as against the eye and the mind, the vision of limited vision is pegged fast in all its dual import.

The poetic imagery of the tragedy plays a role of many parts in presenting and illuminating its complex theme and interwoven body of meaning. The images give particularity and vividness to the expressions of the characters and shade-in undertones of their thought and emotion. They help to prepare for, or foreshadow, developments of attitude and action. On various occasions the imagery functions to create specific contrasts between the attitudes of divergent characters, as they use similar images from different points of view, and in this way there is created a high degree of verbal tension and of emotional intensity. In their symbolic functions the master-tropes deepen the frame of reference and help to bring into the perspective the larger issues within which the temporal action takes place. But it may be re-emphasized that it is because these dominant images are closely integrated into the structure of the play that their general symbolic effects are valid for the play. The symbolic values of the dominant images are, in fact, developed by a skillfully modulated progression so as to come to full effect as interconnected sequences rather than as simple type emblems. As the imagery deepens the awareness of various implications and attitudes running through the play on more than just the surface level, the images also work to establish emotional and imaginative connections from incident to incident of the plot. And by a kind of backward reference in the later part of the tragedy elements of the imagery serve to render particularly intense the folly and shortsightedness which have been displayed, as the dominant images, like the *phronein* motif, twist back against Creon. Yet it is more than a question of the images reinforcing and decorating the theme. The very multiplicity of response exacted by the images, especially as handled at critical points in the action and as related to Creon, infuses the feeling of a tragic breach between the apparent and the real through the whole tissue of the poem to make it part of the poem's life blood. Multivalence of language is here related closely to multivalence in life. Things are not always as they seem on the surface. Many of the facts and many of the problems which men face involve not just one meaning or one clear and right solution. They are ramified in their meanings and values, to pose a most difficult problem for men who are, we are made to feel, morally responsible but often incompetent intellectually.

> Far-roving hope is to many men a boon and to many the deceit of airy desires. Disillusionment comes to one who knows not until he burns his foot in the hot fire. (616-20)

# POSTSCRIPT · APPROACHES TO THE ISSUE

## *The General Problem*

SINCE at least the time of Aristophanes, Sophocles' style has drawn acclaims of over-all excellence even while it has posed a paradoxical problem for critics endeavoring to explain to others the qualities of his expression. Technique and content are one in a subtle and unmistakably sure control of the powers of language, or, as one recent writer has put it, the language from Sophocles' stylus was a "molten flow . . . fitting and revealing every contour of meaning, with no words wasted and no words poured on for effect."[1] As a result the purity, clarity, pattern, balance, and harmony of Sophocles' expression are all but academic commonplaces. Unfortunately, as in the case of moral goodness, these qualities are hard to define, and when talked about too much they come to seem very dull. So in the case of Sophocles it is almost as though an unusual degree of formal control and a much admired subtlety of craftsmanship have created a style so lacking in striking idiosyncrasies that critics must be repeatedly thwarted in their efforts to deal with it adequately.

Such things as the exuberant imagery and "heavy compounds" of Aeschylus or the rhetorical niceties of Euripides somehow seem to offer firmer ground and a surer way into the very center of those authors' styles than any elements in Sophocles' diction. Many interpretations of Sophocles' style have, in fact, taken the form of describing the more marked peculiarities of these other two of the Attic triad, against which Sophocles' facility is viewed as a median kind of excellence and is described in negatives. To some, Sophocles' seeming lack of distinctive stylistic detail has made his poetry seem conventional, monotonous, "classic" in the worst sense.[2] But the record of such adverse verdicts is relatively small. The great majority have accepted the judgment of "Longinus," who ranked Sophocles as one of the great, intense and daring) (as against the flawless and pretty),[3] and then most have turned to other elements of his dramas which more readily admit of analysis than does his mode of expressing thought in language.

In general one can distinguish two groups among the relatively few studies which have been made of Sophoclean diction and style. The first kind is highly analytical and tends to a quantitative cataloguing of grammatical and rhetorical forms. The latest of these studies is ambitiously entitled, *The Style of Sophocles* by F. R. Earp (Cambridge, 1944). Starting with a desire "to ascertain, if possible, how and why the style of Sophocles is so surpassingly good," Earp offers tabulations of certain types of words and figures of speech for each of the seven plays. From these counts he draws limited conclusions, mainly that the diction becomes progressively more natural and "dramatic" and that one can make a chronological arrangement of the plays on this basis. Carefully worked as are most of these studies and important as they are for basic lexicographical matters, they tend to slight the fact that a poet's language is vital and functions in context. Style is only in a very limited sense a product of quantities of verbal forms. Of this group of stylistic compilations, Lewis Campbell's introduction to his edition of Sophocles' plays is by far the most comprehensive, and it goes well beyond most others in efforts to show the purposefulness which Sophocles exhibits in his use of rhetorical figures and his moulding of grammar.[4]

At the other extreme are what can generally be classed as appreciations, more descriptive and evaluative in form. Usually short, they tend to appear as lectures and minor chapters in general books on Sophocles or on Greek tragedy, and here one is almost sure to find either uncomfortable generalities or, at worst, open-mouthed rapturing. One of the outstanding among this group is J. W. Mackail's essay in his *Lectures on Greek Poetry*. The acuteness of observation and illustration in this impressionistic essay merit more than faint praise. But prominent in it are such effusive and vague terms of excellence as these: a preeminent sense of language, purity and sense of form, a sense of quietness and certain unaccountable lustre, in clear faultless pattern the miracle of life, Pheidian, the embodiment of Hellas (at its best). Usually less well expressed than by Mackail, the tendency to the broad generalization dominates many efforts to describe Sophocles' poetry; yet, terms such as these, generally true and no doubt sincerely used, are usually only satisfactory to the man who writes them. They offer little assistance to the reader who faces the central question of what makes Sophocles' poetry act on him in a compelling way, with suggestive, expanding force, instead of as flawless, patterned verse. Moreover, today generally harmony and simplicity, like sweetness and light, are terms which have been drained of content. They are no longer adequate to convey the intensity and depth and dynamic resolution of complexities which Sophocles' poetry contains.

These characteristic difficulties of criticism with Sophocles mark the clashing rocks between which current criticism must find a way if it will advance the understanding of his dramas.[5] On the one hand we must avoid large appreciative generalities and simple admiration of mere pattern or form in the large sense. We must penetrate past formalness and technical excellence in general to the elements of the poetry which constitute its intense, vibrant, and meaningful qualities. The danger on the other side is the tendency of detailed analysis of the elements of the poetry to become only quantitative and to lead to oversimplifications and distortions of fact by removing material too radically from its original contexts. Much remains to be done to chart this course in all its aspects. But the most productive way is, I believe, one which will base on the significant (rather than simply the distinctive) elements in Sophocles' expression, will examine these closely in relation to context, and work out through structural and connective factors of the context to the larger significances of part and of the whole.

## *Imagery* : *A Working Definition*

⟨The imagery employed by Sophocles is a functional means of communication in his dramas. It is aesthetic not simply in the sense of the decorative, but in the true sense of being a means of perception (*aisthêsis*) offered to the reader by the poet to take him into the meaning of the work⟩ This is a basic hypothesis of this study. To be sure logicians have repeatedly protested against figurative language, as for example Hobbes who declared that "metaphors and senseless and ambiguous words are like *ignis fatui* and reasoning upon them is wandering amongst innumerable absurdities" (*Leviathan*, 1, 5). But imagery and purposefully ambiguous words remain facts of poetry and of human experience without which Hobbes could not have written this particular sentence. We must try to deal with them in positive terms despite the difficulties they present to the mathematical approach and the rational mind. If, then, in seeking a definition of imagery we are stepping onto a *pons asinorum* or entering a No Man's Land where all sorts of specialists wage fierce guerilla warfare, yet for our purposes a brief marking out of the limits of our primary subject may save us from some errors and help us to keep our subject firmly on this side of "the borderline of sanity."[6] Because of our distance in time from the language of fifth century Athens we cannot hope to treat it with the freedom or the inworking subtleties which can be applied to the language of most English poets. We require certain simplified guides as to what we can and cannot justifiably do in our endeavor to analyze the play's total structure through the leads given by its images. For this purpose it will be sufficient here to outline a general working definition applicable to the study of Sophocles' practice in the *Antigone*.

For the purposes of this study the term imagery denotes what is often called "figurative imagery"—i.e. basically metaphor and its related forms. A restriction such as this aids analysis against becoming lost in overly intricate details and channels attention to those forms of imagery which are most intrinsically kinetic because they comprise a relationship of dissimilar elements in one or another of several ways. But, as is now general practice, "imagery" is not limited to figures that appeal only to the sense of sight. Within our province are any use of concrete, sensuous terms which are not simply descriptive but which are so used as to communicate emotional attitudes or intellectual perceptions indirectly, either by a transfer of meaning or by analogy. Thus we are including what rhetoricians distinguished as metaphor proper, synecdoche, metonymy, personification and "the enlivening of lifeless things."[7] It seems also proper to include the exemplification of a general observation by concrete analogy in any case where the expression is both concrete and suggestive. A good example is the second ode (Stasimon 1) of the *Antigone*. The general observation, "wonders are many and none more awesome than man," is not proved but is elucidated and deepened by the series of concrete illustrations drawn from various provinces of human activity. After the first line of the ode, the effect at any instant is not simply the opening generalization nor the series of descriptions simply as factual descriptions; the effect is compound.

The images with which we can deal most readily are what might be termed substantive images, those which offer a sensory term or a term drawn from the material order of things. This includes images drawing upon various major human pursuits and institutions of which our knowledge can be said to be fairly concrete and objective—for example, farming, warfare, the home, and for the Greeks certain aspects of a rich mythological tradition. Elements drawn from such areas of experience are sufficiently public property and sufficiently constant to provide concrete and substantive reference when introduced in metaphors. On the other hand, more unstable in content and often too fine for our net are emotional and intellectual "images," those which draw directly on feelings, on psychological phenomena, on abstract concepts, or on literary allusion as the vehicles of expression. Such kinds of expression are of course not lacking in the play nor without genuine structural significance for it, and in the final chapter we have drawn upon the evidence of the dominant image sequences to probe also into these additional aspects of the language in their major, detectable bearings for the structure.

But at this point a distinction needs to be made between the subject matter and effect of imagery. Though we can conveniently class certain images as substantive or objective in respect to the area from which they draw their particular referents, imagery as poetically used is almost always prejudicial or normative in effect. That is, poetic images represent or convey an attitude, feeling, or judgment and give to this a quality of precise particularity because of the seemingly objective terms in which they put it. In this respect the images of poetry can be distinguished from the language of science or what is sometimes called "pure prose."[8] Fire and silver have only the most limited meaning in the mineral "pyrargyrite." The grammarian who first distinguished German verbs as "strong" and "weak" obviously did not want to convey their respective power in straining students of the language. The language at a poet's disposal obviously contains many such terms which may once have been concrete and metaphorically active but which by usage have been generalized or so altered that they are faded, dead, or neutral as images. In the *Antigone* a few of the many examples are the use of *pous* ("foot") for the sheet of a sail and numerous of the manual and physical terms applied to mental processes. We shall come back to this point, and in the examination of the play we must be alert for the way in which Sophocles often reenlivens such terms, but generally speaking, dead and neutral metaphors belong more to the study of language in general than to our purposes.

In this study, then, we are concerned particularly with figurative poetic imagery that utilizes a sensory or substantive reference and that is normative or emotional in effect. Such images involve at least two terms. One is stated and concrete; the other more general and possibly only implied.[9] For example, when Teiresias says to Creon in 994, "Therefore you used safely to pilot (*enauklêreis*) the city," the explicit concrete implies guiding and ruling. But in the examples already cited from the second ode both terms are explicit, as they are also in such similes as that applied to Antigone by the Guard:

> The girl looked and wailed the shrill cry of a bitter
> bird as when it sees its nest empty. . . . (424-5)

In many cases the statement of the concrete element may lie in overtones of words, in connotations rendered active by context. An elementary example is the opening of Creon's first speech (162-3), where the metaphor of the ship of state is recognized by all even though the ship is not mentioned and the word which most directly implies the sea, *salos*, not infrequently means something else: any tossing motion, as of an earthquake, the condition of general perplexity, and also the rolling swell of the sea or the tossing of a ship at sea. Roughly the two terms involved in any figurative image may be compared to two overlapping circles made to impinge on each other by the poet so as to focus on the area of their mutual coverage. The primary term, the *vehicle*, is usually concrete or sensory; the other term, the *tenor*, may be conceptual or emotional. The effect of the image, and this perhaps requires special stress, comes from the interaction of the two elements.[10] The relative prominence and extension of vehicle and tenor vary greatly in different instances, but the compound effect is definite even in such simple synecdoches as the Chorus' query to Creon:

> Will you murder (*kteneis*) your son's marriage? (568)

and Teiresias' warning,

> Stab (*kentei*) not the dead. (1029-30)

Literal action with a sharp instrument of the hand is not expected from Creon in either case, nor yet do the words convey only a remote, abstract idea of destruction. The effect, as we have repeated cause to see, is often multivalent as well as compound. Here one of the simplest examples may again suffice. When Haimon says that Antigone is considered worthy of "golden honor" (699), the connotations of brightness, monetary worth, general value, long lasting quality and possibly others as well, are active simultaneously. There is no need to settle on just one meaning so long as the complex relates to the context.[11]

## Formal Characteristics of the Images

Every image in the play to some degree aids in establishing tone, evoking feeling, or shading in undertones of thought and emotion. The forms in which the images are cast also contribute to tone and convey quality of thought. In a sense these factors, the value of individual images in limited context and the formal characteristics of the imagery, belong to the texture of the structure. But one's appreciation of these factors will condition one's understanding of Sophocles' practices in those elements of the imagery which contribute more directly to the advancing, interacting structure of attitudes and issues.

For the study of structure the classical distinction of metaphors and similes from synecdoches and metonymies may at first glance seem beside the point, since it involves chiefly a difference of degree in the same kind of effect and is largely a matter of intensity in the specific instance. But the differences which these terms denote in the form and employment of images do have a mass effect of sorts. It is obvious, for example, that there are fewer images in the dialogue portions of the *Antigone* which bridge a radical gap between species of existence than in any Aeschylean play or any equivalent number of lines from Pindar. If one insists upon being startled at the poet's fusion of dissimilars in metaphor, it is even possible for analysis to reduce Sophocles' "figurative language" to the status of being sporadic and insignificant. F. R. Earp's listing is the most extreme in this direction, crediting only twenty-four metaphors and seven similes to the *Antigone*.[12] Such a limitation presents a distorted picture. Vital images are not lacking in the play, but many are subtle in the way they infuse the particular with the general, and a large proportion which draw upon elementary bodily processes could best be classified, formally speaking, as synecdoches or metonymies. In translation they are likely to seem like clichés, but a few may be cited as typical of many:

Hot is your heart for chilling deeds. (88)[13]
There is no shame in honoring those of the same flesh as
   oneself. (511)
This is not reverence, to trample the honors of the
   gods. (745)
You have laid hands on my bitterest grief. (857)

One hesitates to assign a number to the images of this type
for practically nothing about images submits to exact count,
and one could dispute at length about the degree of concrete
force in each instance. But as a type they are many, and the
cumulative effect of this practice must affect even the casual
reader. In general, the tendency to employ images whose
terms have natural and common connection results in making
Sophocles' language seem less coruscant and daring than that
of such poets as Aeschylus, and by the same means Sophocles
also may be seen to hold attention closely and consistently
to the dramatic subject.[14]

The paucity of formal similes in the play is particularly
significant. There are only twelve, including four comparisons which might more strictly be classed as short parables or
allegories.[15] Two appear in odes. Of the others, only one is
of any length and calls for an extended projection of the
imagination by the reader. This is the simile in which Antigone likens herself to Niobe, and it appears in a semi-lyric
kommos:

How often I have heard the story of Niobe,
Tantalos' wretched daughter, how the stone
Clung fast about her, ivy-close: and they say
The rain falls endlessly
And sifting snow; her tears are never done.
I feel the loneliness of her death in mine. (823-33)[16]

The others in the dialogue are clipped and direct, giving
clarity and concreteness to an emotion or a principle. The
Guard tells of his first view of Antigone at the corpse and
voices his sympathy, not very boldly, by the simile of a bird
crying over its empty nest (424-5). Creon drives home the

need of the weak to yield to the strong by two parables (874-8). Haimon later balances this with two parables illustrating the need even of the strong to yield on occasion (712-17). And in the simile of the eagle in the first anapestic system of the first ode special care seems to have been taken to translate the exact relationship envisioned between the eagle and the Argive host (both streaked with white and plumed) before a much more complex, indirect and metaphorical working out of the image is undertaken in the following antistrophe.[17]

Similes are not, of course, invariably simple or unsuggestive, but the directness and almost pictorial clarity of the similes in this play, together with their scarcity, provides a fairly sure guide to what Sophocles was not aiming at in his use of imagery through the rest of the play. The far more extensive use of metaphorical forms, with their basic indirection, is generally true of Attic tragedy. But even if one would assign this fact to a "tragic convention," as against the "epic convention" of extended simile, the elevation of metaphor, with its manner of implication and suggestive identification, over simile, with its usually explicit exactness, appears to seek and achieve effects of rapidity and intensity together with the possibility of extensive associations.

We may perhaps approach the values of these procedures in the play more fully by viewing them in another way. There are obviously a great many ways by which poetic images may take their departure from neutral or literal comparisons. In this play there are notably few which do so by an exuberant and extended development of the vehicle. The Niobe simile and the description of the storm for the action of the gods in the third ode (Stasimon II, 582-92) are about the only ones so formed.[18] On the other hand, most frequent are images in which metaphorical meaning is indicated but in which an exactly defined picture is not offered or, if suggested, is not sketched in precise outline. For lack of another name we may term them sunken or latent images.[19] This manner of imagery is by no means confined to this play or to Sophocles, but it is the basic procedure here, and in its various manifestations merits close attention, for it seems often to have escaped attention.

An excellent example involving one of the basic tropes of the play is Creon's expression of the force of the god upon him as he finally comes to realize it after the catastrophe:

> Now surely some god struck down on my head, con-
> straining me with great weight. He drove me into wild
> ways, overturning my joy so that it is trampled down.
> O my woe! (1272-5)

Here we can if we wish trace out some of the suggestions of the lines by rephrasing the vehicle as follows: "Now surely some god leaped upon me and drove me hard over wild ways so that like a stallion gone mad under blows and too sharp a curb I overturned my joy and trampled it." The image at once becomes more restricted, more clear, less fruitful in its context. As we get it in the play the references to horse-driving lie partly in connotations. Holding heavily, striking, driving, wild ways, trampling—all offer such suggestions, partly because of previous exploitation of animal imagery in relation to Creon. There is also some suggestion of the fairly common Greek notion of a supernatural agent swooping down from the heavens. The image is further enriched and intensified because the terms *agriais hodois* (wild ways) and *lakpatêton* (trampled down, trampling down) compress several levels of meaning. The "wild ways" may be unmannerly or unreasonable conduct; they are equally rough roads or severe terrain over which the (implied) horse is being driven. The adjective *lakpatêton*, as I have shown elsewhere, is both transitive and intransitive and refers either to the action of the god or of Creon himself. In this image, then, feelings of force and emotional anguish are strongly realized and rapidly conveyed at the expense of simple visual or grammatical clarity. In its hinted, compacted multiplicity the expression is more accurate than any paraphrase in setting the confusion and elements of bitter recognition within Creon's mind at this point in the play.

Other examples of the same sort are in the first ode, where

a rising and submerging and shifting of images of horsemanship together with a suggestive extension of the conflict
between the eagle of Argos and the snake of Thebes help
to create the sense of terrible struggle and dark danger just
passed. In the first antistrophe (117-27) the metaphorical
extension of the eagle-snake conflict is extremely indirect.
The presence of the snake is, in fact, introduced only by the
word *stoma* (mouth, or any entrance or outlet, 119); it is
then given further sunken expression within the phrase,
*toios amphi nôt' etathê / patagmos Areos*; and only in the
last word of the strophe is the symbol of Thebes made explicit. A full translation would have to render these final lines:
"So great around [the eagle's] flanks there curled and con-
strained the din of War, the terrible subduing handiwork
of the dragon adversary."[20] But this involves using slightly
over two words for every Greek word to catch the multiple
suggestions, and it involves being graphically detailed where
the poet is being pregnantly suggestive. As these sunken
images raise suggestions and stimulate the imagination, they
create their effects of vague apprehension or ominous warning and lead to a feeling of depths below the surface partly
just because they do not fully satisfy the sense of sight.[21]

Extreme compression of image is another manifestation
of the imagistic mode characteristic of the play. The exultant,
shouting, torch-bearing rites of the Maenads, for example,
are packed in the phrase *euion te pur* ("and the blaze of the
Bacchic cry," 964). The legend of Capaneus is called into
the play in the first ode by virtually a single word, *pyrphoros*
(firebearer, 135). And not infrequently the images are in the
overtones of a word or expression. The main denotation,
that is, makes adequate prose sense, but associated meanings
or connotations add range and vitality in ways which because
of context cannot be regarded as merely accidental. For example, when Antigone repudiates Ismene's effort to share
her guilt and terms her Creon's *kêdemôn* (guardian, or
patron, 549), there is certainly a further active overtone besides the surface sarcasm. The word as it is originally used
in Homer is applied to signify persons attending the dead;

it is at least indirectly connected with family duties; and so it connotes here the very kind of special attention that Antigone, in distinction from her sister, has given to her brother's corpse. Quite a number of these latent images, which perhaps might be specified as images of overtone, figure in the dominant image sequences and are illustrated there. See, for example, in the animal sequence the images in *aneimenas* (579) and *phorbê* (775).

In other instances imagery which has been introduced more explicitly is effectively sustained in latent form or an image may be initiated in sunken form to lead up to a more direct statement. The latter way figures, for example, in one of the key images to which we recur several times in the study of structure, 289-92. There are sunken allusions to the effect of the yoke in the phrases *molis pherontes* (bearing a heavy burden) and *kara seiontes* (tossing their heads) before Creon makes explicit in the last line his telling identification between his citizens and beasts of burden.[22] Another example is in Creon's first speech. The opening figure of the ship of state, itself relatively clear though set by implication, is sustained in latent form (as in 168 and 178) for a considerable time to re-emerge more strongly in lines 189-90. A similar subtle use of an image to bracket a speech and infuse it, as it were, from both ends occurs in Creon's speech of counsel to his son, 639-80, and in this case the quietly controlled, and initially almost casual, vehicle of the soldier in ranks has, we come to see, deep-reaching, reflective undertones for our understanding of Creon's principles.

The suggestive and sure effects which Sophocles attains by a restrained and sunken employment of the image vehicle are to a considerable extent part and parcel of our main study. But in respect to general characteristics, the numerous simpler kinaesthetic expressions which couple concrete verbs with abstract nouns are also part of this manner of sunken imagery. It is, in fact, a pervasive kind of practice for the play which colors the tone of the whole. Criticism has often observed that these various less obvious and nongraphic uses of imagery seem to be particularly adapted to reflective and

113

thoughtful language, and in particular Wells and Pecz, dealing respectively with the Elizabethans and the Attic tragedians, have maintained that partiality to such forms of imagery marks the contemplative mind and conveys the quality of matured thought.[23] Without pressing to extremes it is indeed reasonable to see this practice as instrumental in the general qualities of quietness and reserve so often attributed to Sophocles' style. What we get in the various sunken and latent uses of imagery in this play is an extremely close fusion of the general and particular. Tenor and vehicle are often not distinctly separable, and, generally, the sensory elements of the images are not drawn either emphatically or in sharp detail. Yet the expression does not surrender particularity to generalization or fail to use the concrete to give telling substance to the abstract. Rather, the many sunken and latent images of the *Antigone* work into the texture of the play a vital controlled intensity which arises in part just from their quality of being implied rather than directly stated, felt rather than seen. Many times hinted comparisons are the most potent, and Sophocles is one who repeatedly capitalizes on a subtle form of imagistic concreteness which gives his language both an aura of precise tangibility and active elements of meaning that extend beyond the simple level of the general tenor.[24]

We must recognize frankly that in many cases there is a question of how much an apparent vehicle term retains concrete basis and metaphorical life—how much, that is, the expression may be faded or neutralized through general usage. When we see in Shakespeare an expression such as this (*Caesar*, ii, i, 132):

> But do not stain
> The even virtue of our enterprise,
> Nor th' insuppressive mettle of our spirits,

we are likely to relish the image at once. But with the Greek terms *miasma* and *miainô*, as in 171-2, 776, 1042-4, the chances are that the concrete sense of "stain" has already been lost in a general notion of defilement. There are, as we have said, numerous other cases where there is simply no objective, lexicographical criterion for this problem. Does *tarassô* (to stir up, trouble, disturb) in the play still act metaphorically when applied to mental conditions? Or is it as dead as its English equivalents from the same root: "trouble" and "perturb"? Even though we learn from dictionaries that such words may have been applied to signify general qualities well before the time of Sophocles, our decision often cannot be certain, for most of the evidence available is from poets and the use we have to determine is a poet's use.

As I have illustrated in chapter 1, context is here a most important guide. When we find the poet recurring repeatedly to a word or image and working observable changes with it, we can be quite certain that the term is by no means dead. This is the case repeatedly in the image sequences of the *Antigone* and is a factor which, in part, frees us from the limitations of inadequate lexicographical knowledge and leads us to center on the recurrent tropes for the study of the play's imagery. In numerous other instances also context gives us fairly certain indications that the poet would have us be aware of the metaphorical potentialities of common expressions: as, for example, when Creon in 1045-6 obviously plays upon the physical sense of the cliché "to *fall* into trouble" which Teiresias had offered him in 1026-7, or when the Messenger likewise exploits the weight of Eurydice's "too *grave* silence" to reinforce its ominous qualities (1251 and 1256). In our study we have restricted ourselves to cases in which such factors of immediate context or significant recurrence can guide us. But finally we may add to these illustrations an *a priori* principle: poetry is concrete. If we err in regarding too large a proportion of Sophocles' vocabulary as concrete, we are at least leaning in the direction of the poetic imagination.[25]

## Subject Matter of the Images

In choice of subject the images in the *Antigone* are not new. They are related closely to a general poetic diction which Sophocles inherited from Aeschylus and other predecessors extending back to include Homer. One can, in fact, find at least one precedent for every image that appears in the play, and this appears also to be true for Sophocles' other plays.[26] This is obviously not as immediately damning a fact in a classical author, for whom tradition and conventions of diction were always important, as it is likely to seem to those accustomed largely to the English Romantic Movement with its high regard for the new expression and the image-making faculty. But the fact is occasionally turned against Sophocles by classicists who are devotees of Pindar and Aeschylus and who would stress the "imaginative" power of these two great masters as it is shown in their ability to find new realms of association and illustration.[27] This limitation in Sophoclean imagery should instead direct attention to the way in which he uses images and makes them function to his purposes. It is not stretching the meaning of Coleridge too far to observe that even this foremost of the Romantic theorists viewed the use and functional adaptation of images as far more important than their individual beauty, or their truth to external nature, or the novelty of their subject.[28]

Certain images appear so repeatedly in Greek tragedy as to be almost formulae for certain situations. Among these are the use of winds for a change of fortune, waves of the sea for trouble, agriculture for procreation and growth, the goad for grief or love, the yoke for necessity or slavery.[29] In the *Antigone* Sophocles trades to a considerable extent on the sea and its storms as concrete referents for trouble (e.g. 162ff., 541, 584ff.). The snake appears once in traditional fashion for underhanded activity (531). The expression of unexpected calamity in a heavenly avenger swooping down is standard (1345-6). And the dominant images generally have a basis in familiar association. It is, in fact, just because the images he employs were to some extent established and known that Sophocles could so often be indirect and subtle in his employment of them. If it is true, as is likely, that the featuring of graphic simile over metaphor by Homer reflects his position in helping to create and make familiar Greek literary diction and that Aeschylus' later full employment of metaphorical indirection is dependent upon a wider general familiarity with a well-established literary diction, then Sophocles' tendency to hinted and sunken forms of imagery is a third step of advance.[30] But in considering Sophocles' images from this standpoint one cannot mark off any as pure symbols. Many of the more or less stock subjects are variable in application or may be said to offer different facets of symbolic reference depending upon how they are used. In the *Antigone* these images take their values from the circumstances of their use, from the contextual relations which the poet has established, almost as much as they give certain constant elements to the expressions in which they appear. For example, the yoking and breaking of animals is a thing of wonderful accomplishment in the second ode, but in lines 289-99 this same vehicle tends to mark a man's tyrannical frame of mind. Gold represents arrogance in 130 but great and real worth in 699. Of basic importance in the dramatic conflict is the way in which the two chief antagonists employ the same images for quite different meanings. Still, the partial extent to which the most frequent images do tend to convey certain common attitudes or certain familiar associations provides analysis with a valuable aid for the recognition of the complex, and often only hinted, relations which exist between images in the play.

In range of subjects the images of the play represent most provinces of normal experience for an Athenian of the fifth century B.C. Predominant in number are images from the sea and ships, from animals and animal culture, from military life, from trade and commerce, from the home, and from health and disease. The greatest single category is formed by images of bodily action (including the five primary senses) together with personifications. Less frequent are those from physical substances, plants, religion and legend, and those which seem to have been proverbial. The span is fairly normal, except that there are almost no images which definitely draw on Athenian public life and institutions. This lack seem particularly strange in view of the extent to which the conflict of the play involves questions of law, of leaders' powers and of individual rights. In part it may be explained by the "dramatic date" of the action, but there may have been in fact a good deal more specific legal reference than we can now recognize. The ground is generally unsure in this sphere, for our knowledge of fifth century legal terminology is very scanty, and many terms known as technical in fourth century Attic law are only general terms given specific application. No one can say if *haliskomai* in 46 suggested "to be convicted and condemned" as well as simply "to be caught," or if one should take the words in 399 with which the Guard turns Antigone over to Creon as something like "accuse and convict her" instead of the less sharply foresighted "question and examine her."[31] In most cases the specific legal or political sense, as it might be recreated from later uses, is not opposed to the general sense. But our evidence is so uncertain that it is best to admit the limitations even though it means that we are missing a factor of the imagery which probably proved of special interest to the original audience.

A considerable degree of prominence accrues to what I have termed the six dominant images or master-tropes of the *Antigone* through frequency of recurrence, but it is the effective employment of them in relation to each other and to the total scheme of the play which makes their frequency finally significant. In grouping these images into six sequences we must recognize that the images at times overlap or tend to fuse two or more of the sequences. The limits of each image are not in each instance exactly definable. Even the designation of six major groups is to some extent arbitrary, for it is possible to subclassify and rearrange groupings on the basis of subject matter. As I see the play, these six sequences most closely conform to the highly functional organization of the *Antigone*, and they seem best to permit the inspection of the interworkings which the poet has created between the various images of the play.

From Aristophanes' *Frogs* we can gather that the quantitative mode of criticism flourished as early as the fifth century B.C., and it quite properly drew a certain amount of mockery from this first of recorded literary critics.[32] Specific counts and tabular treatments of Sophocles' imagery are to be found,[33] and to a certain extent, as has been illustrated, the preponderance of certain imagistic practices has a genuine bearing in the interpretation of the play. But such counts belong more to the raw efforts of research than to its proper products, for they not only oversimplify but often seem to imply that literature can be subjected to scientific weights and scales. Any attempt to count and catalogue images precisely is bound to be arbitrary, since (1) no two people are likely to agree in each instance whether an expression is figurative or not, (2) the effect of even a strongly developed image is likely to be somewhat different for any two people and may lead them to classify it under different subjects, and (3) some images do not belong solely to one class or another but may belong to several at once. Systems of computation can be applied which recognize and endeavor to minimize these differences. In such cases as Miss Spurgeon's treatment of Shakespeare they can be illuminating to the study of an author's personality or for developments in his style, but only if accompanied by enough nonarithmetical qualification and comment. In the case of Sophocles, such tabulations are of almost no assistance biographically.[34] The semiconventional range of the subject matter militates against biographical incursions into his imagery. The tabulating approach, too, has so far proved of little value in furthering the understanding of Sophocles' style except in respect to the raw material of his diction. It seems prudence, then, to welcome the complexity and richness of the material and to seek to appreciate the positive assets of these qualities of the imagery. The images of the *Antigone* are not so many static ciphers or even so many fixed verbal forms of such and such kinds. The important consideration is not exactly how many images there are but how the leading images act, in what ways they interact, how they relate to the whole and help it convey its meanings, which, because it is a work of art, are complex and often intangible.

| | PROLOGUE | PARODOS | EPISODE I | | STAS. I | EPISODE II | | | STAS II |
|---|---|---|---|---|---|---|---|---|---|
| | | | Creon's edict | First Guard sc. | | Second Guard sc. | Antig. and Cr. | Ism., Antig., and Cr. | |
| MILITARY IMAGERY | 8–10 (27) (32–4) (87) 62 | Military subject | 168–9 215–7 | 241–2 296–7 | | | | | |
| IMAGERY OF THE SEA | 20 83 | | (159) 162–3 167 178 188–90 | (259) (290) | 334–7 | | | 536–7 540–1 | 582–9 615–6 |
| IMAGERY OF ANIMALS AND THEIR CONTROL | 29–30 | 105–9 110–26 131–3 139–40 (149) | 201–2 205–6 (241–2) | 257–8 289–92 | 338–41 342–53 | 423–5 432–4 | 477–9 | 531–5 579 | |
| IMAGERY OF MONEY AND MERCHANDISING | 29–30 | | 175–7 221–2 | 293– 303 310–2 322 325–6 | | | 461–4 | | |
| IMAGERY OF DISEASE AND CURE | | | | | 363–4 | 419–21 | | | |
| IMAGERY OF MARRIAGE (with Death) | | | | | | | | 568–75 (581) | |

(N.B. Underlining indicates images regarded as of distinctive importance in each sequen parentheses mark images of least vitality outside immediate context and those whose relation a sequence is indirect.)

| EPISODE III | STAS. III | EPISODE IV | | STAS. IV | EPISODE V | | STAS. V | EXODOS | |
|---|---|---|---|---|---|---|---|---|---|
| Hai-mon-Creon | | kom-mos | Cr. and Antig. | | Teiresias sc. | Cr. and Chorus | | Msgr. and Euryd. | Creon |
| 639–40<br>668–76<br>688–9<br>740 | 781<br>799 | | | | 1033–5<br>1084–6 | 1096–7<br>1106 | | | |
| 675–6)<br>715–7 | 785 | | | 954 | 944<br>(1000)<br>(1058) | | (1117–8) | (1162–4) | 1283–5 |
| 775 | 791–2<br>800–1 | | | 946–7<br>955<br>985 | 999–1004<br>1021–2 | | (1124) | 1214<br>1231 | 1272–5 |
| 684<br>699 | 782 | | | 950 | 1032<br>1035–9<br>1047<br>1055–6<br>1061–3<br>1077–9 | | | 1168–71 | 1326–7 |
| 732 | | 817–9 | | | 1015–7<br>1026–7<br>1052<br>1080–3 | | 1140–5 | | 1283–5 |
| 653–4<br>77–80) | (Love's vitality is the theme)<br>802–5 | 810–6<br>833<br>867<br>876–7 | 891–2<br>916–20 | 944–50 | | | | (1167)<br>1204–7<br>1223–5<br>1240–1 | |

Notes

# NOTES

## CHAPTER I. INTRODUCTION

1. A convenient summary of the divergent views concerning the central issue of the play and the question of the "guilt" of the two chief characters is given by M. K. Flickinger, *The Hamartia of Sophocles' Antigone* (Iowa Studies in Classical Philology, no. 2, 1935), pp. 19-42. A more compressed summary pointed to what I feel is a more significant conclusion is given by P. J. B. Egger, *Das Antigone-Problem* (Solothurn, 1906), pp. 47-54, 67-8.

2. C. M. Bowra, *Sophoclean Tragedy* (Oxford, 1944), p. 114. H. D. F. Kitto, *Greek Tragedy* (London, 1939), pp. 123-8, gives an excellent analysis of the play and a view of the theme which is more strictly ethical but in many ways similar to Bowra's. He virtually cuts out the religious element and substitutes a "way of life" as the criterion of the insight and blindness of the characters.

3. R. B. Heilman, *This Great Stage* (Louisiana State University Press, 1948), p. 4. This very able and rewarding study of imagery and structure in *King Lear*, which appeared after the major part of my essay had been written, offers in its first chapter a thorough presentation of the critical principles which underlie my study also. Heilman has developed these methods incisively and has applied them to *King Lear* with a degree of subtlety and control which is probably not to be matched for a Greek tragedy.

4. *On the Sublime*, x and xxxivff. To an excessive degree ancient criticism starting with Aristotle tended to separate the verbal (as decorative) from elements of thought (as subject for decoration). See, for example, the emphatic statement of this distinction by Dionysius of Halicarnassus in *De compositione verborum*, 1; also Horace, *Ars poetica*, 333-46. This tendency was of course not absolutely maintained, and it is less present in "Longinus" than in almost any other ancient critic. Allen Tate in the *Hudson Review*, 1 (1948), pp. 344-59, ventures that Longinus "came nearer to a comprehensive theory of literary form than any other ancient critic."

5. W. B. Stanford, *Greek Metaphor* (Oxford, 1936), *Ambiguity in Greek Literature* (Oxford, 1939), *Aeschylus in His Style* (Dublin, 1942). The first two books give a thorough treatment of ancient critical theory followed by analyses of the practice of the Greek poets, particularly Homer, Pindar, Aeschylus, and Sophocles. The interpretative

sections show beyond any question how poets then as now went their creative ways, leaving to Aristotle and later theorists "the placing of too much emphasis on the logical functions of language." In his *Aeschylus*, pp. 96-102, Stanford traces out some of the dominant recurrent images of the Aeschylean plays. These analyses are, I feel, useful preliminaries, for in none of them does Stanford probe as deeply or profitably into the image patterns of the plays as needs to be done and as Stanford himself comes closer to doing, in chapters x and xi of *Ambiguity*, with the *Agamemnon* and the *Oedipus Tyrannus*. In a very thorough and revealing recent study, *The Io Allegory of Aeschylus' Suppliants* (diss., Princeton, 1949; not yet published), R. D. Murray extends and corrects Stanford's analyses of the basic patterns of that play. The presence of a significant symbolic sight pattern in the *Oedipus Tyrannus*, which is sketched by Stanford in *Ambiguity*, pp. 170ff., is described at more length and used as a comparison for Shakespeare's method in *King Lear* by Heilman, *op.cit.*, pp. 20-4. The initial step toward the interpretation of recurrent imagery in Greek tragedy seems to have been taken by W. Headlam, with perceptive remarks on Aeschylean metaphor in *Classical Review*, 16 (1902), pp. 434-42.

6. E. Fränkel, "Aeschylus: New Texts and Old Problems," *Proceedings of the British Academy*, 28 (1942), p. 251. The article is concerned more with textual problems and the clarification of some critical loci in the plays than with the larger objective which the given quotation sets forward.

7. M. E. Prior, *The Language of Tragedy* (New York, 1947), p. 11, supplies the quotation. He treats only English tragedy, but the congruence of his findings in Elizabethan drama with the findings of this study is, like Heilman's book, strong confirmation of the existence of common potentialities and techniques in the imagery of the best poetry of different ages, especially when language is in the hands of such masters as Shakespeare and the Greek tragedians.

8. *Poetics*, vi.

9. See in particular *Poetics*, ix: "Poetry, then, is something more philosophic and of graver import than history, since its statements are of the nature rather of universals, whereas those of history are of singulars."

10. *Poetics*, xxii: "But the greatest thing by far is to be a master of metaphor . . . since a good metaphor implies an intuitive perception of the similarity in dissimilars."

11. Jebb's Greek text (see bibliography) is used as the basis for readings and interpretations except where I indicate otherwise. Any translation is a partial interpretation. In some cases I may seem to overtranslate or stress by translation what may be just a partial or secondary meaning

of the Greek. This is intentional, but when done the notes indicate other possible interpretations or further levels of meaning. In a few cases expressions are translated slightly differently in different places to try to bring to bear different elements in the richness of the original language.

12. For a fuller treatment of this kind of submerged imagery which at first looks almost like a cliché, see pp. 110-15.

13. 454-5: The term *hyperdramein* seems usually to have meant "outracing," but the obvious contrast with Creon's words is almost certainly intentional and brings up suggestions of riding over as well as of riding past a limit. This seems to be recognized in Jebb's translation "override."

14. The bearing of these images within this ode are treated more fully in chapter IV.

15. 1272-5: The key word for the transgression-trampling sequence is the adjective *lakpatêton* (trampled with the foot, trampling with the foot). It is both passive and active and refers ambiguously to the action of the god or to Creon as the agent. That we are to recognize the daemonic action referred to in these four lines to be the result of Creon's error and not its primary cause seems very clear from his direct acceptance of responsibility in 1262-9 and from the whole Teiresias scene.

## CHAPTER II. THE IMAGERY OF EVALUATION AND CONTROL

1. The word here as in 1037, 1047, and 1061 is *kerdos*; also in 222, 311-13 (twice), 326, 461-4 (twice) and 1326 (twice). Often denoting general advantage or gain rather than monetary or other concrete profit, its use in close connection with Creon's two very vivid monetary images (295-303 and 1035-9) and with his repeated charges of bribery leaves no question that the concrete as well as the general sense of the word is to be felt in the various appearances. In this particular scene the merchandising image may be felt to start in 994 ("Therefore you used to pilot the city safely" and/or "Therefore you used to manage the ship of state safely"); for the verb *nauklêreô* seems often to have meant in the fifth century B.C. "to be a ship owner" instead of "to pilot" or "to be a ship's captain."

2. In 294-5, *nomisma* functions in the double sense of (a) custom or anything sanctioned by usage and (b) its special meaning of currency or current coinage.

In 300-1, the word-play between *panourgia* (commonly: villainy) and *pantos ergou dyssebeia* cannot be caught in translation. The same word-play with a strong ironic bite appears in 68 and 74, where against Ismene's caution not to be overly active, Antigone replies that she will be ὅσια πανουργήσασα, i.e. "ever active in pious works" and "villainous for holy ends." The echoing of this pun in Creon's speech is a nice subtle touch recalling the two points of view.

3. 29-30: *glykyn thêsauron*: The Scholiast's explanation *hermaion*, *heurêma* (lucky find, or simply: thing found) indicates the general tenor of the expression, but it is significant that this is one of few instances where Antigone speaks in substantive metaphorical language, and the more vivid potentialities of the image have a place in the cumulative sequence of monetary images which follows. Schneidewin and Nauck, *Antigone* (9th ed., Berlin, 1886), bracket this line with a characteristic free hand because they feel that the use of the term *thêsauros* for the prey of birds to be "extremely unusual." But that is no valid cause for expurgation here. The straining of the term, if felt, is likely to indicate an effort to compress several levels of emotion or perception into one image, which is surely the case here.

4. 461-8: The twofold repetition of *kerdos* is a partial key that the word is being stressed and would seem sufficient cause for recalling the contrasting implications of Creon's recurrent use of the term and of other monetary images in the preceding episode.

5. The Messenger in trying to express the general application of the catastrophe does so in terms of wealth and substance and presents Creon's life as no longer worth appraisal: "Let a man, then, amass great treasures in his house if he wishes and live with tyrant's pomp. But if with all this he loses happiness, I would not pay any man the shadow of a vapor for all the rest, compared with joy" (1168-71). The final echo appears when Creon has expressed his realization of his error. As he terms himself worth nothing at all and asks to be led away (1325), the Chorus replies, "There is profit in this counsel, if any profit can be found in troubles" (1326).

6. The concluding lines of Antigone's speech quoted last above more or less epitomize for our attention this recurrent generation of division and misunderstanding between the two protagonists through their use of common terminology of valuation and judgment from diverse points of view: "If I seem to you to be caught in deeds of folly, it may be that I am judged a fool by a fool!" (469-70).

H. Weinstock, *Sophokles* (Leipzig, 1931), pp. 103-5, has shown how the separation of the opposing sides is rendered acute by their different uses of the key words "love" and "hate." The process permits simple expressions to carry a tension and feeling of depths below the surface. It is a vital and poetic interanimation of language achieved, I believe, even more particularly and intensely within the image sequences than with the terms of "love" and "hate."

7. Lewis Campbell, *Sophocles* (Oxford, 1879), 2nd ed., vol. 1, note *ad loc.*, also points to the allusion to spurious coinage here. The verb *phainô*, basically a term of vision, aids in setting the concrete basis of the image. There are a good number of diverse and sometimes much argued precedents in Greek poetry for the notion that the friction of time and events provides the test of a man's genuine worth, just as friction applied to metals can in various ways test their purity or strength. The general familiarity of this conceit is without doubt one reason we find the image here offered by suggestion without detailed delineation of the vehicle term.

The most common use of the conceit seems to have been in the form of time the touchstone, which drew upon the practice of rubbing gold on a special kind of stone (the Lydian stone) to obtain a fine streak whose color could then be tested against the streak left by metal of known purity. (Cf. Herodotus, vii, 10; Theognis, 417, 449, 1105, 1164; Pindar, *Pythian*, x, 67-8; Bacchylides, Fr. 25 [Edmonds]; also Theophrastus, *De lapidibus*, 45-7.) But in at least one early example, the technical use of the touchstone appears to have been replaced by the idea of rubbing down to show what is under a surface coating. This is Simonides, 199 (Edmonds), where Time is the touchstone that shows a man's inner mind (*hypo sternois . . . nóon*). There is also the much commented image in Aeschylus, *Agamemnon*, 390-3. If one does not try to bind the image there too closely with the touchstone (which is not mentioned, though usually assumed by commentators), the vehicle of Aeschylus' image seems to be the exposure of black, inferior copper (*kakou . . . chalkou*) after the surface of something is worn off by repeated rubbing (τριβῷ τε καὶ προσβολαῖς). I venture to posit that this something in the *Agamemnon* passage and in both Sophoclean expressions which we are considering is " 'bad money,' having a core of copper and plated with silver." That such was not unknown to the Greeks of the mid-fifth century b.c. is attested by Charles Seltman, *Greek Coins* (London, 1933), pp. 108 and 138. (But for other "solutions" which are more complicated in their efforts to remove or retain the touchstone in the Aeschylean passage, see Fränkel, *op.cit.*, pp. 251-2; G. Thompson, *Classical Review*, 58 [1944], pp. 35-7; Sinclair and Eichholz, *Classical Review*, 59 [1945], p. 52.)

8. 1078: *katêrgyrômenos* (literally: plated with silver): The Scholiast again shuns the image and explains the term as simply "persuaded by money." Jebb, as on most occasions, also inclines toward a monosemantic interpretation, noting that the participle here figuratively means "bribed"

though the term properly denoted "overlaid with silver." In the few other recorded uses of the verb it always has the concrete meaning of "cover with silver" (Herodotus, I, 98; Diodorus, I, 57). The related adjective *katargyros* appears only later but then also to denote "silvered" or "covered with silver." Of the ancient sources, then, only the Scholiast on this passage gives the meaning "bribed" and the antiquity of his views are open to question. Pindar uses metaphorically a somewhat similar term, *hypargyros* (properly denoting, "having silver underneath" but also "silver-plated"), of a venal voice in a context where there is no reason to assume, any more than here, that the metaphor is dead. In sum, then, lexicographical evidence is too scanty to fix on one and only one meaning for Teiresias' expression, even if poetic technique were so to indicate. What lexicographical evidence there is points to the concrete basis of the image and so to its vitality as a metaphor which carries the concrete and general at once. And we may note here the reappearance of the manual term *tribê* and the visual term *phanei* in connection with image, just as in previous appearance.

9. Note the stress on *cheri* (hand) in 43, which very likely was accompanied by a dramatic gesture, and which is later caught up in 546 and 771.

In 80, the verb προὔχω may also contain a military suggestion. Literally meaning "to hold before," it is used of a shield and spear and, possibly with metaphorical flavor, is used also for offering excuses or pretexts. Most of the martial terms in the prologue might be regarded as neutral were it not for their recurrence and interplay which arouse positive connotations for the scene and the larger context. Thus Ismene's term *macheomai* (to war) in 62 is at least as old a metaphor for verbal argument as Homer, *Iliad*, I, 8 and 304.

10. 241-2: *stochazei* (aim, shoot), *apophragnysai* (block, shut off, bar passage to): Both have well attested military uses. Some editors seek to bring the two images closer together and interpret both as metaphors from hunting. As noted in various editions, Pollux states that *stochasmos* and *stoichismos* and several related nouns were used to describe the setting of hunting nets, and Xenophon uses the verb *stoichizein* in this sense. For this interpretation the images may be rendered, "You set the nets carefully indeed and hedge the approaches all around" as if preparing a trap for game (viz. Creon). But the simpler use of *stochazomai* as to "aim" or "shoot at" (and hence sometimes to "endeavor" or to "guess") is much better recorded for Attic Greek, and it fits with Creon's later use of a similar archery image in a stronger context, 1033-5.

11. 640: *opisthen hestanai*: The phrase appears to be idiomatic of occupying a position in ranks. See references in Jebb's note *ad loc.*; cf.

NOTES

Campbell, *ad loc*. See also *Ajax*, 1249, where Agamemnon to Teucer uses the inversion of ranks as an image of anarchy or disorder in a context where he (Agamemnon) clearly stands for an erroneously autocratic point of view negating valid feelings of humanity and religious duty focused in the unburied body of Ajax.

12. Equivocally the man who does not break the laws and the man who rules the state.

13. 670-1: The terms *prostassô* and *parastatês* appear to be, respectively, the regular expressions for placing soldiers in ranks and for one who stands next to another in ranks.

14. In 674 emendations of the manuscripts' σὺν μάχῃ do not seem to benefit the sense. Campbell sensibly keeps the manuscript reading as "vivid," i.e. "Disorder helps with battle to make utter rout." There seems to be no genuine reason to limit the preposition to the sense of "aiding," which is the basis of Jebb's objection; it means simply "in company with."

The translation of 675-6 may overtranslate, for the idea is generally: Obedience saves the lives of most whose course is upright. But the concrete object *sômata* (bodies) tends to tie the expression back to the vivid martial personification, and the primary notion of straightness and order in the participle *orthoumenôn* has the same effect.

15. Cf. O. W. Reinmuth, *The Foreigners in the Attic Ephebeia* (University of Nebraska Studies, no. 9, 1929), p. 8. It now appears that there is no objective evidence for the existence of the Attic ephebeia, the regularized two-year period of military training, prior to 335/4 B.C. Therefore Jebb's explicit identification of the terms in 670-1 with the terms of the later ephebic oath is only partially valid, and perhaps not at all germane to the interpretation of this passage.

16. See 733-9 where Haimon forces into the open the contrast of democratic and autocratic principles. An excellent perspective for the education and training of Attic youths in the fifth century is afforded by Thucydides, II, 39, 1 and 4, in the principles that the historian has Pericles express there. He contrasts the Athenians' excellence in war, despite very limited training, with the Spartans' laborious discipline to the end of creating an efficient military machine. Like this play, Pericles' funeral oration (in its civic rather than its imperialistic elements) seems to express a deep-seated Athenian opposition to autocratic power and to the regimentation of citizens by an individual or by the state beyond the limits necessary for general order and progress. This can be said without raising the more limited and probably unsolvable question of whether Sophocles was for or against the Periclean party.

17. Compare 296-7 and 673-4 for particular responsions within the general parallelism of the two personifications.

18. 688-9: *proskopein* (often: to look ahead, foresee, provide against): The military sense of "to reconnoitre" or "spy out beforehand," here perhaps connotative, appears as definitely denotative in Euripides, *Iphigenia in Aulis*, 1098, and Aristophanes, *Knights*, 154. The bearing of the military signification here, from out of the broader range of the word, is signaled by Creon's images and also by the stress on *skopoi* and *proskopoi* in 215-17. The image forms a deft touch such as may now be seen to be characteristic of the play; for in trying to win his father's attention Haimon again is made to call upon his father's mode of imagery. But Haimon does so to suggest that as Creon's son he is not just any soldier in Creon's ranks but rather an advance scout (zealous, daring, and well informed) in his father's interest.

In these lines I believe we should retain the reading, σοῦ δ'οὖν πέφυκα, the first reading of Ms. L. It is not only the *durior lectio* but also the richer expression, for the genitive σοῦ has a double value. In the first part of the sentence, the sense is: "My nature inherited from you, as your son, is . . ."; but, as the sentence unfolds further, the genitive also acts with the infinitive, *proskopein*, to give us: ". . . to look ahead (scout out) in your behalf."

19. 1038: *apraktos* (literally: unworked, unworkable) in its concrete or tactile sense continues the archer image, i.e. not hit or not assailed by the arrows of the seers. At the same time, in its sense of "not put to profit" or "unprofitable," it prepares for the following mercantile image. The sense of "to intrigue against" often present in the active verb *prassein* is probably a further level of meaning to be felt in this expression, i.e. *apraktos* as "free of intrigue from." Cf. Campbell, *ad loc*.

20. 1086: *bebaia*, both "firm" or "fixed" as well as "unerring."

Most commentaries seem to conceive these archer similes of the play as images of sport rather than warfare, but cf. G. Lueck, *De comparationum et translationum usu Sophocleo*, part 3 (Stargardt, 1882), p. 10. We can perhaps only be guided by context, which in this case certainly gives us a human target and makes clear that the vulnerative power of the bow is the significant basis for these two similes as the poet chose to develop them.

21. 1095-7: *eikathein* in the general sense of "to yield" is certainly the main denotation, though I have chosen the concrete translation. In this play the term *eikein*, in the sense of yielding to higher authority or greater power, approaches being a minor verbal motif, and rather unusual runs of images are twice built on the term (472-9, 710-8). However, the use of the term in military contexts, as to retire from com-

bat, is well attested: e.g. *Iliad*, v, 606, xii, 48; Herodotus, ii, 80. The other term *anthistêmi* and its forms are particularly used in battle contexts, as for example in this play in 518, though it, too, has a broad general range. Cf. Campbell, *ad loc.*, for the "stroke of Calamity."

Jebb sees the vehicle of the image in these lines as a torrent (of ruin) rushing down on the stationary Creon, who presumably in this interpretation is standing like a tree, for Jebb cites 712. He might also have cited 1103-4 where there is a suggestion of evil men, like trees, falling before the axes of the gods. I would support the convergence of these connotations here but urge that the image is sunken and suggestive rather than exactly pictorial, and that therefore the expression serves to support or carry also the military overtones raised by the immediately preceding bowman's simile and prepared for by Creon's recurrent tendency to use military terms.

22. The foreshadowing, through overtones and undertones in the various speeches, of attitudes and lines of action that later develop explicitly is of course closely related to the familiar and more obvious "Sophoclean irony" of the *Oedipus Tyrannus*, where Oedipus' words again and again point to the certain catastrophe or to the true nature of his dilemma in such a way that the audience is made to realize and foresee these factors even though the characters do not. The difference is largely that in that play the "irony," the ominous meaning of the expressions in the light of the larger context, is more explicitly developed in action and has a more certain external basis. Thus the error of Oedipus' sight and the existence of a more genuine insight, which is effectively developed by verbal imagery, is also doubly reinforced by "imagery of action" in the Teiresias scene and in Oedipus' final self-blinding. And in *Oedipus Tyrannus* the nature of the legend, as well as the dramatic sequence of events, makes more immediately apparent the need of the reader to hold denotations and connotations in his mind simultaneously. The difference in the *Antigone* is that the ambivalence and multivalence of language is less directly supported by the facts of the basic legend or by the sequence of the action in its initial stages. This means that the full significance and richness of the *Antigone* is somewhat more a matter of language and verbal structure and somewhat less the major charge of the plot structure than is the case in the *Oedipus Tyrannus*.

23. *Ajax*, 1253-4, and *Electra*, 1462, afford close parallels. In the latter, Aigisthos' openly tyrannical rule is expressed by him as an imposing of the bit and bridle. In the former, Agamemnon, as he tries to maintain his orders and discipline against Teucer's determination to bury Ajax, threatens with the image of a large ox kept straight in the road by a small goad.

NOTES

24. 206 (literally: mangled to see): The construction is strained. Whether one reads the masculine or neuter form of the participle, the sense is little changed, and the final phrase injects a last violent, visually concrete element into the expression. See also 1040-3 where Creon commits the body to the eagles of Zeus. Contrast Antigone's fear lest Polyneices' body become carrion (29-30) and Teiresias' barbed warning that it is not for animals to "hallow" the corpses of men (1080-3).

25. The one-sidedness as well as the vehemence of Creon's expression is highlighted by contrast with the immediately preceding sympathetic images used by the Chorus to greet Ismene: the cloud of grief and fond sisterly tears which mar her face (526-30).

26. 578-81: μηδ' ἀνειμένας: Jebb, in his comments on *Ajax*, 1214, recognizes the reference of the term to consecrated animals as the commonest denotation of this passive participle, but for some reason he ignores it here and limits its bearing there (cf. Heredotus, II, 65, and Plato, *Critias*, 119D). This use of the term is paralleled by a similar meaning in the adjective *aphetos*, which Aeschylus has Io use with particular appropriateness in the *Prometheus* and which Aristotle cites as a particularly energizing metaphor: *Prometheus*, 666; *Rhetoric*, III, xi, 2 (*re* Isocrates, *Philip*, 127).

The general tenor or prose sense of the first two lines would seem to be: "Servants escort them inside. Hereafter they must be women and not let loose [to escape]." So the Scholiast. Both Campbell, *op.cit.*, vol. I, p. 454, and Jebb, note *ad loc.*, emphasize a social denotation, a reference to the fact that Attic propriety forbade to women such freedom as Antigone has displayed. This seems indubitable, but it would seem to be taken care of thoroughly in the main clause, "From now on these two must be women," after which the phrase *mêd' aneimenas* might even seem sheer padding if the social implication were all. As it is, the positioning of the phrase—set off by a verse caesura, almost dangling at the end of the sentence and more or less superfluous to the main prose sense—catches attention and invites fresh associations along the lines already established by the imagery.

27. 775: *phorbê* (animal fodder, though also applied in the fifth century to food of any kind): Observe that in the *Philoctetes* the term is used repeatedly of Philoctetes' plight, which is in many ways animal-like (e.g. 43, 162, 712, 1107). In the *Ajax* it designates the food of wild birds, while Homer uses it only for the fodder or forage of animals.

28. 131-3: *balbides* (the rope marking the start and the finish of the race track): In Greek poetry outside this passage, where the reference is to the battlements of Thebes, there is no recorded use of the term for other than the goal of a race until much later.

134

29. 106-9: The reading ὀξυτόρῳ (piercing, galling) instead of ὀξυτέρῳ (swifter, sharper) is the first reading of both major manuscripts, L and A. The Greeks seem to have urged their horses to full speed by shaking the reins hard (e.g. *Electra*, 713, and *Antigone*, 1274) and this must have affected the bit. Thus the original reading of the older manuscript, which gives us a "galling curb," includes the ideas both of speed of flight and of strong, severe control. Helios (the Sun) in semi-personification is then the driver. The Scholiast simply notes ὀξυτέρῳ, ὀξεῖ, both of which, be it noted, are ambiguous terms including the meaning "sharp" and, more dominantly, the meaning "swift." Some later manuscripts have taken the first of these terms into the text, and most editors have accepted it. The word χαλινῷ (bridle) then has to be taken as generalized into "career" or "pace," so that the two terms together form a dative of manner showing the speed of flight, i.e. "in headlong flight with swiftened pace." Against this traditional view there are several other points. For metrical and grammatical reasons it seems difficult to separate the two datives from the participle which they bracket (ὀξυτόρῳ κινήσασα χαλινῷ). To take them as a dative of means with the participle and its implied agent seems most natural, i.e. "driving with galling curb." The tactile image of control in *oxytoros* also better fits the context of the ode. The first strophe includes a definite semi-personification of the sun, and at several other places in the ode the gods are presented as active in horsemanship. The familiar role of Helios as a charioteer is external evidence to substantiate this interpretation.

30. 1272-5 The vehicle of the image is partially submerged. The references to horse-driving lie partly in connotations: the blow on the head, holding heavily, striking, driving, wild ways, and trampling. Cf. M. A. Bayfield, *The Antigone of Sophocles* (London, 1901), note on text *ad loc.*

31. 791-2: For the basis of this metaphor and that of the next example in horsemanship see Jebb, *ad loc.* Translation is based on the version by Dudley Fitts and Robert Fitzgerald, which here catches nicely the psychological paradox of the Greek *dikaiôn adikous phrenas* (the unjust minds of the just).

32. 800-1: Translation and interpretation are difficult here. Our knowledge of exact and varied significations of the word *thesmos* (generally: law) is inadequate. But from the form of expression there appears to be some element of contrast here between the *thesmoi* alone in these lines and *hoi megaloi thesmoi* (the great laws) two lines above. Otherwise the repetition must seem confusing or simply pointless.

I interpret as follows: The deification of Love in the main body of the ode seems to imply that "the great laws" are connected with the

135

unwritten, immortal laws of the universe to which Antigone has appealed (450-6). Generally in the Attic tradition these universal, unwritten laws include loyalty to parents as well as, and perhaps even more regularly than, the claims of burial. Thus there can be a conflict between the claims of the *megaloi thesmoi*, viz. Antigone's duty to her brother versus Haimon's duty to his father. In describing the powers of Love in the ode, the Chorus sets forward in mythical and psychological form the existence of possible paradox in the final order of things; equal place beside "the great laws" belongs to Eros with his powers of tenderness and destruction, life and death, sport and ruin. The ode does not deny the divergent demands created within the sphere of "the great laws"; it asserts the reality of certain elements of conflict all through the universe, transcending human control and understanding. Against this, the appearance of *thesmoi*, without the adjective and as something from whose path one may withdraw, seems to refer to the laws and ordinances of men: such as, Creon's edict and perhaps the Chorus' lawful position as the loyal council of the rulers of Thebes. These lesser *thesmoi* the Chorus is here moved to regard as of secondary importance, at least for the time being.

33. Chapter iv. pp. 64-74.

34. Other minor appearances of the imagery are 317, 423-5, 432-3, 827 (*damasen*), and 1307.

35. 1231-2: Cf. W. H. Johns, "Dramatic Effect in Sophocles' *Antigone*, 1232," *Classical Journal*, 43 (1947), p. 100, for another who recognizes the bestial reference here. The power of speech, we also recall, is one of the marks of man in the second ode (354-6).

36. Note also that immediately prior to the parting of father and son, Creon had lashed at his son with this sentence: "Woman's slave, don't wheedle (*kôtille*) me!" (756) The ability of *sainô* in 1214 to echo the notions of coaxing and flattering in this earlier expression, when coupled with Creon's earlier propensity for animal terms, seems to provide further contextual grounds on which to feel here some of the potential vibrancy of the term *sainei*—specifically, its connotation of "fawning," "fawning like a dog."

## CHAPTER III. THREE SUPPORTING IMAGE PATTERNS

1. To trace the similar sequence in *Romeo and Juliet*, see i, 5, 136-7; iii, 2, 136-7; iii, 3, 1-3; iii, 5, 141 and 202-3; iv, 5, 35-9; v, 3, 92-108.

2. 653-4: The Greek reads both as "leave her for someone to wed" and "let her go to wed someone."

3. 802-5: This is a case where context immediately brings out the special connotations of marriage in *thalamos* and *pagkoitês*. The particular designation of a marriage chamber by *thalamos* is familiar; in the adjective *pagkoitês* (generally, "universal sleep producing") there is also *koitê*, the bed and especially a marriage bed.—On the side, it is worth observing how the expression here again compresses into a further unity the paradoxes which make up the ode on Love: tenderness and destructiveness, grief and happiness, life and death.

4. 816: *all' Acheronti nympheusô*: Possibly "wed to Acheron" (the river in Hades personified). Most editors take it so. The locative dative is equally possible, in which case an indefinite person—Hades (812, 1205) or potentially Haimon—is the implied groom. The translation tries to open both possibilities as the Greek line does.

5. A. Patin, *Aesthetisch-kritische Studien zu Sophokles* (Paderborn, 1911), pp. 4ff., sees the stage action as well as the music as representing a bridal procession: first torchbearers to show the way into the dark prison, then servants with bread and wine, then Antigone heavily veiled. Patin takes Antigone's repeated laments for her lack of marriage hymns as referring to the accompanying music which reminds her of them. While such a staging would seem to provide effective integration of dramatic devices with the poetry, deductions such as those of Patin involve interpreting emotional and imaginative images as stage directions and must be somewhat suspect. An excellent discussion and examples of the fusion of the poetic imagery with "the language of props, the language of setting, and the language of action" in poetic drama are to be found in Alan Downer's "The Life of Our Design," *Hudson Review*, 2 (1949), pp. 242-63.

6. The great volume of comment on whether or not this passage, 904-20, or parts of it are genuine hardly needs augmentation. Stylistic arguments are inconclusive; arguments based on a supposed borrowing from Herodotus (III, 119) can be pointed either way; the possibility of an actor's interpolation remains a conjecture, not a certainty. Aristotle knew the passage and cites the most questioned part of it as the proper kind of argument to support Antigone's unusual trait of character—namely, her devotion to her brother over anyone other (*Rhetoric*, III, xvi, 9). The final basis of all arguments is whether the speech is in keeping with Antigone's character as previously depicted. In the Victorian view that Antigone is all radiant and untroubled purity, the lines have been regarded as spurious. In the now more prevalent view that her character is more difficult and also more humanly real, her emotional toil and somewhat illogical argument here have a valid place. The consistency of this speech with Antigone's mode of expression and manner of thought

elsewhere in the play is illustrated more specifically in the final chapter.

7. The suppression of a developed erotic subplot in the *Antigone* is the more noteworthy because of its probable prominence in the lost Euripidean version. Cf. Aristophanes of Byzantium's prose argument for the *Antigone* (Jebb, *op.cit.*, pp. 3-4); Carl Robert, *Oidipus* (Berlin, 1915) 2, pp. 381-95; Max Pohlenz, *Die griechische Tragoedie* (Leipzig, 1930), pp. 190-4.

8. 1207: *akteriston amphi pastada* (literally: from the region of that chamber which had received no funeral rites): Here again there is a tight compression of the two elements of the sequence in a single phrase: *pastas* sometimes having a special meaning of "bridal chamber" and *akteristos* specifically denoting lack of rites due the dead. Cf. Jebb, *op.cit.*, appendix p. 263, on the various meanings of *pastas*.

9. 1224: The phrase *eunês . . . tês katô* also implies "bed (or bride) only to be found in death"; cf. Campbell, *ad loc.* The course of the Greek sentence strengthens this implication. One is offered initially *eunês apoimozonta tês katô*, "wailing (wails) for his bride below." Then, the subsequent accusatives, when they appear, become grammatically the direct objects of the participle. The strict grammatical interpretation is "bewailing the loss of his bride who had died, his father's works and his ill-fated bed."

10. Kenneth Burke in an article "The Imagery of Killing," *Hudson Review*, 1 (1948), pp. 151-67, discusses and illustrates with Milton's *Samson Agonistes* the poetic process of defining "the essence of a motive narratively or dramatically (in terms of *history*) by showing how the motive ended." In the *Antigone* we should bear in mind that Antigone never mentions Haimon or refers to him; the bridegroom she foresees is Hades or some indefinite being (816), who for being indefinite may of course be Haimon. Their union and its consummation in death more closely defines Haimon's motive. To balance the degree of life in death won by his son, Creon becomes one who is dead in life, "a breathing corpse" (1164-7).

11. 732: τοιᾷδ᾽ ἐπείληπται νόσῳ: The verb also carries the metaphor; cf. Herodotus, VIII, 115, and Thucydides, II, 51. By a specialized development the same verb is the basis of our term epilepsy.

12. 1017: *plêrês* (literally: full): Like its synonyms *anapleôs* and *mestos*, it often bears the sense of "infected" and so helps sustain the imagery. See also 1052.

13. 1023-7: In the last two lines the phrase, *es kakon pesôn* (to fall into trouble), coming with the verb *akeitai* (cure, cure oneself) strongly suggests the idiom *es noson pesein* (to fall ill). This extension of the

image vehicle in the Greek may justify a certain overtranslation in the rendering "sluggish" for *akinêtos* (unmoving).

14. Cf. strong initial use of disease imagery for this view in *Oedipus Tyrannus*, 25-7, 68, 150, 169, 217, 303-7, and its extension *re* Oedipus, e.g. 1293 and 1455-6.

15. 615-16: Jebb and Bayfield in their notes on the text both comment on the mariner image, citing Pindar, *Olympian*, xii, 6: "the hopes of men are oft tossed up and down, ploughing a sea of vain deceits." Extended sea imagery in the first strophe of this ode further vitalizes this image. The active sense of the adjective *polyplagktos* (much deceiving, or: causing to err greatly) is also a connotation fitting the immediate context but is probably not the only, or even the primary, meaning.

16. 20: καλχαίνουσ' ἔπος: The primary denotation of the verb seems to be one of color, "to be purple" or "make purple," for it is apparently formed from *kalchê*, a sea mollusc that was a source of purple dye. But the verb is also thought to be influenced by the analogy of *porphyrô*, as used by Homer to express the agitation of the sea and of mind but as also related to *hê porphyra* (the purple murex, also a source of dye) and the adjective *porphyreos* (surging, lurid, purple, dark). Therefore most editors credit the expression here with a double sensuous burden, "to be dark and troublous, like a stormy sea," and scholars disagree only as to whether the notion of dark color or deep stirred agitation is primary. A valuable brief study of intersensal or synaesthetic metaphors in Greek poetry is included in Stanford, *Greek Metaphor*, pp. 47-62.

17. 83: *eksorthou* (guide straight, correct, steer out of trouble): Campbell's note on the term here is appropriately "as if steering a vessel." The terms *orthoô* and *orthos* (with notions of both straight and upright) appear in nautical images in 163, 167, 190, and 994. Like the term σώζω (to save) these words and their compound forms appear to have been common in nautical terminology; cf. Jebb's note on 189.

18. 536-7: εἴπερ ἥδ' ὁμορροθεῖ (most literally: even if, as the fact is, she rows by my side, i.e. is my partner in the deed): Not only the image but the dramatic tenor of Ismene's expression is often taken differently. Nauck's interpretation, *op.cit.*, note *ad loc.*, seems to be similar to that above, and he points up the agreement of metaphors in 536 and 541. Jebb's note recognizes the basic rowing vehicle of the image in both these places, but he then cancels it out both in his commentary and translation. This is done by understanding the word *homorrothei* as meaning "consent" on the basis of the Scholiast's note, *homophônei* (agree). Yet this not only limits us to a small part of the range of the word; it forces the normal use of εἴπερ in tragedy. According to the lexicons this conjunc-

tion with the present tense almost always signifies that the supposition agrees with the fact. This agreement is not the case from the speaker's point of view if one takes the common, Jebbian interpretation: "I did the deed—if she allows my claim." The agreement is maintained if the concrete nautical vehicle is retained in the image and the expression understood as denoting the assertion of actual participation, not merely verbal consent. (Note that the Scholiast on Aristophanes, *Birds*, 851, specifies "rowing together and in time" as the proper meaning of the term.)

In these lines, as here understood, Ismene is sincerely trying to make amends to her sister and offers an emphatic claim of real responsibility, not a weak claim conditional upon her sister's approval. So also later it is Ismene who carries the argument against Creon at the end of this scene (563-73). Within the two lines themselves there is a chiastic marshaling of arguments as Ismene tries to claim the fullest possible amount of guilt. She opens, "I did the deed." But it is apparent that Antigone is there, caught in guilt already. So she voices partnership twice, and then concludes with the stress again on her personal claim (*pherô tês aitias*).

19. Cf. terminology and similar tenor in *Oedipus Tyrannus* 22-4, 46, 56, 101-4, where the image is also the ship of state. The nautical sequence in this other play offers further parallels in its developments for Oedipus: e.g. 420-4 with 1208-10; 921, 1410, and 1527.

20. 593-5: literally, "I see that from olden times the house-troubles of (living) Labdacidae have piled upon the troubles of the dead." But in the opening lines of this second strophe the wave image seems to be carrying on aurally: in the alliteration of 594 and the repetition of words, *pêmata . . . pêmasi, genean genos*. To paraphrase this prosaically, the generations of the house are the storm-beaten headlands, their recurrent troubles are the waves of the sea, the driving power of wind and wave are the gods, in the display of whose action there is unfathomable mystery as well as force.

21. Jebb, *op.cit.*, p. xii.

22. Campbell, in his note *ad loc.*, is almost alone in stressing the concrete vehicle of the image. Jebb and various others take *limên* only as "receptacle" and transfer the adjective *dyskathartos* (as: hard to appease) to the god. Nauck and Bayfield, in their notes *ad loc.*, regard *limên* as "abyss" or "maw," injecting quite extraneous images for no great gain. There is no evidence to necessitate that we regard the image as dead in this context, so that Campbell's interpretation is probably more accurate than those which seek simply to catch the general tenor of the expression. Cf. Aeschylus, *Suppliants*, 471, *koudamou limên kakôn*, "and there is no port safe from (the storms of) evil."

23. E.g. 159, 259, 290, 675-6, 1000, 1162-4.

24. Including of course his confident rejection of superhuman considerations in 280-9 and 1040-4.

## CHAPTER IV. THE ODES

1. 332-3: The diversity of meanings which have been offered as primary denotations of *deinos* in this line is illuminating. For example, Campbell, note *ad loc.*, marks the meaning as "wonderful" on the ground that the word had paused at this point in historical transition from "fearful" to "clever." Jebb, note *ad loc.*, is less explicit as to his reasons but categorically states "not 'dread' nor 'able' but 'wonderful.' " A. B. Drachmann, "Zur Composition der Sophokleischen Antigone," *Hermes*, 43 (1908), pp. 67-8, stresses the sense of "inventiveness" in the term. P. Friedländer, "*Polla ta Deina*," *Hermes*, 69 (1934), pp. 56-63, urges that it denotes "gewaltig," particularly the violence of monstrous beasts and elemental nature such as is presented by Aeschylus in *Choephori*, 585ff. M. Untersteiner, *Sofocle, studio critico* (Florence, 1935), vol. 2, p. 47 n. 35, subscribes to Friedländer's view but adds further implications of the wonderful mental capacity of men as part of the expression. E. Schlesinger, "*Deinotês*," *Philologus* 91, (1936-7), pp. 59-66, argues that the reiterated *deinos* here denotes primarily a human mental capacity that is in itself ethically indifferent, like Aristotle's concept of the capability of *deinotês*. All these views, supported by lexicographical evidence and parallel citations, increase the certainty that in the fifth century B.C. the term *deinos* had a wide range of meaning and that the context must determine what segments of this range are most applicable. The context of this ode supports at least two major and somewhat divergent aspects of these meanings: man's *marvellous capability* and the *strange danger* which it contains.

2. *Choephori*, 585ff., πολλὰ μὲν γᾶ τρέφει δεινὰ δειμάτων ἄχη . . . . κτλ (Fearful things numberless, strange and hurtful breed on earth . . . , etc.).

3. 368: *pareirôn* (usually: weave into, insert). This reading of the major manuscripts, if genuine, includes a forcing of the verb to govern two parallel accusatives and so mean "weave together." This parachresis is defended by Campbell, note *ad loc.*, by W. Schmid, "Probleme aus der Sophokleischen Antigone," *Philologus*, 62, (1903), pp. 21-2, and by Untersteiner, *op.cit.*, vol. 2, p. 48 n. 37. The image of weaving seems an appropriate continuation of the preceding pictures of man's clever handiwork, and the tension in the straining of the term is appropriate for the tenor of the passage.

4. Cf. Schlesinger, *loc.cit.*, p. 66.

5. I.e. "May he never be at my hearth or share my thoughts, the man who does these things" (372-5). The lines refer back to the dramatic origin of the ode, the breaker of the edict; they refer equally, however, to the more general antecedent in the preceding sentence, "the man who because of daring takes to evil."

6. See especially the opposition of the two protagonists over law in 449, 450-60, 480-90.

7. The effect of limited vision and oversimplification in these preceding images is of course increased because when Creon makes his tirade, the audience (though not the Chorus) knows what motivation has in fact produced the burial of Polyneices.

8. 211-14: Both the words *areskei* and *enesti soi* seem to credit Creon with capability rather than approval. The note of tacit disapproval in 213 may not be quite as strong as in the version here used, if the restoration *panti, tout'* (Pearson) is accepted instead of *panti pou g'* (Erfurdt, Jebb).

If further dramatic preparation is felt necessary to support the suggestions of opposition between the ode and the policies and attitudes enunciated by Creon, it may be significant that both the last two responsions of the imagery in the ode are to a speech which forms Creon's last preceding address to the Chorus and which begins with impatient contempt for the Chorus' introduction of a religious cause (280-9).

9. Cf. Jebb, *op.cit.*, p. xii, and also his notes on the text. See also note on 612-14 below, for these are critical lines which are so emended by Jebb and others as to cancel the significance of the elements of the ode which I feel to be central. The imagery of light in this ode appears to have received little critical attention and none as it affects the meaning. W. Schmid, in Schmid-Stählin, *Geschichte der griechischen Literatur* (Munich, 1934), vol. 2, p. 497, refers to the ode as a grand *Helldunkelbild* and suggests a possible connection with the Greek mystery-religions. He does not support the suggestion and perhaps only means to indicate a pervasive "twilight" somberness in the tone of the ode.

10. 599-600: Reading ὑπὲρ / ῥίζας ἐτέτατο φάος (Brunck).

11. 601-2: κατ' αὖ νιν φοινία . . . . ἀμᾷ κόνις: An instance where one is probably forced to remain indefinite as to the exact sense. Jebb, note *ad loc.*, asserts the verb *katamaô* must carry a metaphor of reaping, and various editors emend *konis* to *kopis* to envision a bloody sickle cutting off the root of the house. But the Scholiast offers "hide" or "cover over" as alternate meanings of the verb, and Campbell supports this by other instances in later Greek. The verb *amaô* appears to have a meaning of

"draw together" or "gather," apart from its use "to reap" or "mow down," and the only recorded use of the compound *katamaô* prior to this passage is in Homer as to "heap up" rather than "to mow down." It is probable, then, that the poet used the verb here with a not unintentional dual reference: (1) to terminate the plant image, the root or shoot of the house, and (2) to present the gathered dust as covering out the light. The object, *nin*, is significantly indefinite and furthers this ambiguity.

12. 606: *ho pantogêrôs* (all-aging), Ms. L and the Scholiast.

13. 612-14: καὶ τὸ πρὶν ἐπαρκέσει / νόμος ὅδ', οὐδὲν ἕρπων / θνατῶν βιότῳ πάμπολις ἐκτὸς ἄτας.

These are crucial lines for the interpretation of the ode and ones over which many scholars have disagreed. The emendation adopted (making *herpei* a participle, taking *ouden* as an adverb, and retaining *pampolis*) involves an almost minimum change and seems to be supported by the Scholia. It also appears to carry out the sense of the strophe—i.e. Zeus's rule has this "law": of punishing transgression whenever and wherever met by means of *atê*. The emendation accepted by Jebb and Pearson makes an easily grasped gnome but hardly fits the preceding ideas of the strophe. They keep *herpei*, put a colon before *ouden*, and emend to *pampolu g(e)* for the sense "Nothing that is vast enters the life of men without a curse." This Solonesque maxim has no relation to *hyperbasia* and Zeus's attitude toward it, with which the rest of the strophe seems to be concerned. In the strophe, Zeus's rule and its relevance to human *transgression* have, in fact, the emphatic leading position, and there is nothing to indicate a major change in thought in the middle of the strophe. The phrase, *nomos hod(e)* (this law) is most naturally taken as referring back to Zeus's sovereignty over human transgressors, and not as introducing a different concept of mere greatness as the cause of ruin. Finally, there are the elements of the larger context which make *hyperbasia* particularly significant in this ode and so point against any version of these lines which would cancel its significance. (In the way of possible emendation, one might consider . . . οὐδέ γ' ἕρπει. It does not appear to have been recorded elsewhere but involves a simpler substitution than either of the usual versions given above.)

14. It is not necessary for the interpretation to "see" the surge as white-crested, but in the description it appears as a natural product of the phrase *erebos hyphalon*, literally "the darkness under the surface of the sea." *Erebos* is also a part of the mythic underworld, so that in the phrase there is a suggestion of infernal regions as well as of darkness.

15. Cf. Vergil, *Georgics*, III, 237-41: "fluctus uti medio coepit cum *albescere* ponto/ longius ex altoque sinum trahit, utque volutus/ ad terras

143

immane sonat per saxa, neque ipso/ monte minor procumbit; at ima exaestuat unda/ verticibus *nigramque* alte subiectat *harenam*."

16. The recurrent appearances of *atê* in the ode (584, 614, 624, 625) seem to range in meaning all the way from moral blindness to the misdeed resulting therefrom and the ruin which ultimately ensues, besides probably being colored by the Homeric personification of *Atê* as "the eldest child of Zeus who blinds (*aatai*) all," *Iliad*, xix, 91, 126ff. In this ode the notion of calamity appears to be the primary one near the start, but in the first strophe a semi-animation of *atê* seems present in the participle *herpon* (creeping) and in its presentation as an agent in the gods' activity against the house. A. Buttmann, *Abhandlung über das zweite Stasimon in des Sophokles Antigone* (Prenzlau, 1869), pp. 4-7, gives particular stress to the bearing for this ode of *Atê* as "the daemonic power which punishes man's presumptions."

17. The introduction of *hyperbasia* in this strophe and, in fact, the whole burden of the strophe are sometimes regarded as explaining the original cause which brought the curse to the house of Labdacus. Thus in *La tecnica corale di Sofocle* (Naples, 1928), pp. 75-8, V. De Falco presents the logical structure of the ode as effect (two strophes) followed by cause (two strophes). This explanation, while probably a genuine connection of meaning on the surface level, does not account for what I feel to be important facts within the strophe and bearing upon it from its context in the play—namely, the stress given *hyperbasia* in the preceding episode and its extension as a verbal motif later in the play; its emphatic, lead position in the strophe; the emphasis and highlighting provided by the color imagery. All these factors make the strophe and the topic of the punishment of "transgression" much more intimately connected with the conflict of Antigone and Creon than any act of transgression several generations in the past.

18. 603: The relation of the Erinyes and a curse on a house is of course familiar from the *Oresteia* and partly explains the choice of word here. Observe, however, that Erinys and Atê are associated in *Iliad*, xix, 87ff. and *Agamemnon*, 1433. The Erinyes are daughters of night, agents of the underworld, dwellers in Erebos, and are regularly "dark powers" who, like Atê, may lead men to mistake evil for good: e.g. *Agamemnon*, 462; *Iliad*, ix, 571; *Odyssey*, xv, 234. W. Headlam, "Ghost-Raising, Magic and the Underworld," *Classical Review*, 16 (1902), pp. 52-5, sketches the common split of Greek divinities into "Blacks" and "Whites," the gods of the upper world and the infernal powers, respectively.

19. The specific point of color overlap between the Greeks' use of the terms *kelainos* (properly: black) and *phoinios* (properly: blood-red) is

of minor importance; their common connotations of fatality and sorrow are of more bearing. But see A. E. Kober, *The Use of Color Terms in the Greek Poets* (Geneva, N.Y., 1932), pp. 37-9 and 89-91.

20. 621-24: The Scholiast suggests that this reported saying draws on some traditional maxim such as, "Whom the gods wish to destroy they first drive mad."

21. W. Kranz, *Stasimon* (Berlin, 1933), pp. 218-19, sums up this ode as depicting an objective superhuman force which would destroy us in order to cleanse us and raise us up. This general interpretation seems to me to be much truer to the facts of the ode than Jebb's emphasis upon the theme of destiny and far more valid than the other view of daemonic forces playing a large-scale game with men throughout the tragedy which is offered by K. Reinhardt, *Sophokles* (Frankfurt, 1933), e.g. pp. 78, 82.

22. *Sofocle*, 1, p. 143.

23. For example, it is probable that Sophocles wrote two plays on the Phineus story and may have assumed details of his treatment as background familiar to the audience for the strophes on Cleopatra.

24. I. Errandonea, "Sophoclei chori persona tragica," *Mnemosyne*, 51 (1923), pp. 180-201, and "Über Sophokles Antigone, 944-87," *Philologische Wochenschrift* (1930), cols. 1373-5. The second article alters the interpretation of the second strophe to point up its implications against Creon as well as its hints towards Haimon's suicide.

25. There is probable mention of Eurydice's other son in 1302-5, but it is only a passing mention and refers to an event outside the play, his death during the siege of the city by the "Seven."

26. V. De Falco, *op.cit.*, p. 206, asserts that the stasima always refer to events in episodes which have preceded, not to the whole drama, and only slightly, if ever, to actions that follow. This bold generalization breaks down repeatedly on specific examination, and is not itself adequate cause for rejecting Errandonea's view of dramatic foreshadowing in this ode. Cf. Kranz, *op.cit.*, pp. 26ff. and pp. 209-19, for foreshadowing and extending implications in various Sophoclean odes; also A. L. S. Rahm's extensive analysis, *Über den Zusammenhang zwischen Chorliedern und Handlung in den erhaltenen Dramen des Sophokles und Euripides* (Erlangen, 1907), pp. 26ff.

27. *Op.cit.*, pp. 104-5.

28. 958-60: The line may mean "So terrible and exuberant a power flowed out of his madness," referring to the deeds which got Lycurgus into trouble rather than to the abatement of his madness while imprisoned; cf. Campbell, note *ad loc*.

29. 947: κατεζεύχθη, in association with θαλάμῳ, may also have a

latent forward reference to the action of Zeus as described later and as detectable in uses of the terms *zeugnymi* and *zygos* for sexual union, even though the compound verb is not recorded as clearly so used until Aelian. If this double reference is felt in the image, it may heighten the basic contrast with respect to human and divine agents in the driving images; for though Zeus "yokes" Danaë in the sexual sense, this is a miracle of benevolence and honor (948-50), as against the dark constraint of her imprisonment, which is the primary reference of the yoke (944-7).

30. Cf. "Acrisius" and "Perseus" in W. Smith, *Dictionary of Greek and Roman Biography and Mythology* (London, 1867), 3 vols.

31. Specially Danaë's "tomb-like bridal chamber" (947) in reference to Antigone's imprisonment as death nuptials (804, 813-15, 891, etc.).

32. In 952 the emendation *olbos* (wealth) is generally accepted on the basis of Baccylides, fr. 48 (Edmonds). This makes solid sense. However, if one keeps the *ombros* (rain) of all manuscripts, one has a kenning which includes the implication of contrast between Danaë and Acrisius, for of the four items all she certainly did have was the rain, "the golden rain," and it was through this that "fate" acted most directly on her.

33. 958: πετρώδει . . . . ἐν δεσμῷ (in rocky bondage). The Scholiast explains the phrase as "in the firm bonds of the vine." If this figurative sense of the expression were more definite from a full knowledge of the legend, it would serve further to make Lycurgus' case only a surface parallel to Antigone's imprisonment. But most editors regard the phrase as denoting some sort of cave more directly comparable to Antigone's prison.

34. Piety has been Antigone's chief claim together with affection for her brother. This is, in fact, emphasized in the last line of dialogue before this ode (943). The Chorus, too, has recognized this claim, as against a sense of political expediency, in its next to last comment before this ode (872-5). Lycurgus, on the other hand, is explicitly impious (960-3). And in this play the Chorus' several invocations of the god Dionysus (as a patron of the tragic chorus and as a god most closely identified with the welfare of Thebes, 152-4, 1121-5, 1136) may have the special effect of heightening the degree to which Lycurgus should be viewed as flagrant in impiety.

35. Cf. *Iliad*, VI, 130ff.; Hyginus, *Fabellae*, 132, 242; Servius, *In Aeneidos*, III, 14; Apollodorus, III, 5, 1. The Homeric version is the only one extant that antedates Sophocles. It does not include the madness, but has Lycurgus punished by blindness that soon leads to his death.

36. Observe that Lycurgus is not named; in fact, Danaë is the only

one of the figures named in the ode. This immediately carries us into a realm of allusion. So long as the context lends support there is no reason why one must stop at the primary level of allusion (Lycurgus himself) and not move into a secondary level (the son whom he killed).

37. See 450-60, 519, 579, 749, 811ff.

38. Diodorus, IV, 44, 3.

39. Diodorus, IV, 43, 3 and 44, 4; cf. Scholia on Apollonius of Rhodes, II, 178 and 227. Jebb, *op.cit.*, pp. 173, for example, dismisses the bearing of Cleopatra's sons as follows: "the fate of the sons is made so prominent only because nothing else could give so strong a sense of the savage hatred which pursued the mother."

40. 972-4: Here, that is, *typhlothen*, normally a passive participle "blinded" or "made blind," with *helkos* as its noun has to signify "a wound which produced blindness." Similarly *alaon*, normally meaning "sightless," is also forced into an active signification, "bringing blindness to."

41. 974: *alastoroisin ommatôn kyklois* (the vengeful orbits of their eyes). The adjective is rare, but its noun is common, *alastôr*: an avenger, an accomplisher of vengeance. Campbell, note *ad loc.*, appears also to feel the pregnant implication as he comments, "Pleading successfully though silently for vengeance."

42. Support for this is to be found both in the account given by Diodorus (IV, 43-4) and that in the Scholia on Apollonius of Rhodes, where in each case the story is one of punishment coming to Phineus for his treatment of his sons.

43. In 985 Cleopatra is described as *hamippos* (horse-swift). This minor recurrence of animal imagery, appearing so close to the final expression of the theme of fate, seems partially to revive the earlier image of the yoke of necessity. It may simultaneously reflect the established tension in this imagery between men unjustly yoking men (which her story partly illustrates) and the proper subservience to supernatural agencies, such as Fate (which her story ostensibly illustrates).

44. Cf. Gilbert Murray, *Sophocles, The Antigone* (New York, 1941), p. 11: "in certain passages (particularly 853ff., 872ff.) where their words seem intentionally obscure one is bound to choose the interpretation which favors the condemned prisoner; had they meant to support the tyrant there would have been no need for obscurity."

45. 872-4: The choice and repetition of the term *kratos* (power) for Creon's authority cannot be regarded as accidental in this play where questions of authority and right are so central; for, though *kratos* is not uncommonly used of governmental sovereignty, it denotes primarily authority as force. Cf. J. H. H. Schmidt, *Synonymik der griechischen*

NOTES

*Sprache* (Leipzig, 1876-86), vol. 3, pp. 656-73. If the poet had meant to indicate a less questionable type of authority, various synonyms were available that are metrically suitable: e.g. *archê, nomos, dikê.* Schmidt, p. 673, quotes a distinction drawn by the grammarian Ammonius which seems very appropriate to this play: "To rule (*archein*) is to be set over men for their benefit; but to have power (*kratein*) is to lead submissive subjects by force to slavery. Therefore *kratein* can be applied to the control of animals but never *archein.*"

46. 875: cf. Errandonea in *Mnemosyne,* 51 (1923), p. 192, "*autognôsia* significat perfectam cognitam," and Untersteiner, *Sofocle,* 2, p. 53 n. 79. The word is more commonly taken as "self-chosen," with an implication of willfulness. Both levels are relevant in the context.

47. 853-6: προβᾶσ' ἐπ' ἔσχατον θράσους
ὑψηλὸν ἐς Δίκας βάθρον
προσέπεσες, ὦ τεκνον· πολὺν
πατρῷον δ'ἐκτίνεις τιν' ἆθλον.

This reading involves a minimal alteration of Ms. L.: the grave accent of *polun* and *ektineis* for *ekteineis*. Punctuation is indefinite; this version follows Musgrave. The interpretation offered appears to be supported by the Scholia. Similar ones are presented by W. Schmid, in *Philologus,* 62, pp. 27-8, and Errandonea, *loc.cit.,* pp. 191-2.

Many punctuate with a period ending the third line and accept the later manuscripts' reading *polu,* in the unusual sense of falling "violently," in place of taking *polun* (great) with *athlon* (reward). This changes the sense radically and in Jebb's interpretation makes Antigone a rebel attacking Justice. Against this view that *dikê* (justice) here represents the laws of the state promulgated by Creon, observe the emphatic use of *kratos* in 872 and see my note on it. The numerous other emendations which rewrite the text or accept one or more of other variations found in later manuscripts need scarcely be considered; a sufficient number are listed in the apparatus of Jebb's text and more on p. 236 of M. W. Humphrey's *The Antigone of Sophocles* (London, 1891). A. C. Pearson's free manipulation of the lines in the Oxford text is a stern example of the effort to force upon the lines one and only one meaning and endow the Chorus with a solid unambiguous attitude.

48. Both words, *thrasos* and *prospipto,* have so wide a range of common meanings that their tone can be determined only by context, which in this case is partly ambiguous but not necessarily any more derogatory than favorable in import. *Thrasos,* though often taken as "over-boldness," in itself means "boldness" or "daring" and often has a good sense, as "courage": e.g. in Sophocles, *Ph.* 104, *Tr.* 723, *El.* 995. The use of

148

*prospiptô* as to fall at another's feet or prostrate oneself in supplication appears also in Sophocles, *Aj.* 1181 and *Tr.* 904, and here it may be felt to be specially appropriate because of the reference to the divine statue or altar. The Aeschylean image of the unjust man spurning with his foot, or seeking to kick over, the altar of Justice (*Agam.* 381-4, *Eum.* 538-42) is, however, no guide here though it is sometimes cited as a parallel. The points of resemblance of this expression to that image are too general to demand an exact correspondence, and whereas Aeschylus' image is explicit as to the physical and moral violence of the agent, Sophocles' expression is not.

## CHAPTER V. "AND AT LAST TEACH WISDOM"

1. See also Aristotle, *Poetics*, XIX, particularly 1456ª36-ᵇ7: "Under the category of thought is included every effect which has to be produced by speech"; or as Bywater interprets the lines: "The thought of the characters is shown in everything to be effected by their language."

2. The previous sections have included most of Antigone's more substantive images wherein a more stable and less private kind of subject matter forms the vehicle of her emotion or judgment. They include a few which are highly imaginative, for example, the Niobe simile (823-33) and the personifying invocation of nature (844-9) but a much larger proportion in which the vehicle is sunken and not visually delineated, as in 7-10, 83, 453-5, 461-4.

3. 499-501: *areston . . . arestheiê . . . aphandanonta*. Five direct terms of pleasure and displeasure are concentrated by Antigone in lines 499-507.

4. In this same scene observe also her emotional terms in 519 and 551 and how Creon is made to turn the sentiment of 523 back against Antigone and at the same time echo her sentiment of 73-6 when he answers, "Go then to the world of the dead and, if you must love, love them" (524-5).

5. For example, the concluding epode begins, "Unwept, unfriended, without marriage songs, wretched in mind I am led away . . ." and ends, "For my fate no tear is shed, no friends make moan" (876-82).

6. The parallelism in mode of argument between these speeches has also been noted by R. W. E. Wycherley, "Note on Sophocles' *Antigone*, 904-20," *Classical Philology*, 42 (1947), pp. 51-2.

7. Kitto, *Greek Tragedy*, p. 127, views this possible borrowing from Herodotus in particularly positive terms, describing it as "the finest borrowing in literature." The final stage of Antigone's tragedy is for him summed up in the fact that here in her last appearance she can only cling to a frigid sophism.

8. Bowra, *Sophoclean Tragedy*, pp. 93-6. If we are right in seeing the *nomos-physis* controversy as an issue developed by the Sophists of the latter half of the fifth century into an assertion of the relative nature of law, a matter of *thesis* not of *physis*, then these lines wherein Antigone partially tries to find a basis for her "law" in "nature" seem to belong more to the old tradition than to the Sophists. *Vide infra.*

9. For example, Campbell, *op.cit.*, pp. 453-4; Weinstock, *Sophokles*, 107-8; Reinhardt, *Sophokles*, pp. 75-105 (throughout).

10. Cf. Jebb, *op.cit.*, pp. xii-xiii, and Bowra, *op.cit.*, 48, 64, 70, for external evidence of the attitude of the Greeks toward burial; also N. P. Vlachos, *The Subject of Sophocles' Antigone* (diss., Univ. of Penna., 1901), pp. 7-9.

11. The Chorus' comment on the speech stresses its emotionalism in delivery: "Here speaks the passionate child of a passionate father" (471-2).

12. A strong critical emphasis is placed on Antigone's harshness to her sister in M. K. Flickinger's study of the *hamartia* of the drama, *op.cit.*, pp. 45ff., and pp. 71-3. Kitto, *op.cit.*, pp. 126-8, offers an able statement of the reasonable view between regarding Antigone as spotless and as the vehicle of a major tragic flaw.

13. E.g. 176, 207, 281, 479, 561-2, 640, 727, etc.

14. The verbal motif has been quite thoroughly charted by Charles Knapp, "A Point in the Interpretation of *Antigone* of Sophocles," *American Journal of Philology*, 37 (1916), pp. 300-16. The chief terms on each side are for the rational, *phronein, phrên, ennoein, noun echein, euboulia, gnômê,* and for the supposedly irrational, *mê phronein, anous, aphrosynê, aboulia, dysboulia, moria.*

15. The Guard is also a minor exception, 317-23. In the Haimon scene see especially 705-9 where Haimon cautions his father.

> Wear not, then, a single, self-sufficient temper or assume that your word and nothing else is true. For when a man believes that he alone knows how to think or that he has unmatched sense and power of speech, laid open he is ever found hollow and void.

16. Cf. also 998, 1015, 1023, 1026, 1031, 1050-3, 1060, 1090.

17. There is also a verbal responsion in this confession, especially in 1269, to Antigone's lines in the prologue, 95-6, where she accepts the charge of *dysboulia* and urges honor a higher consideration.

18. Cf. also 288, 291, 494, 508, 1342, and the image of spurious coinage (175-7). The use of visual terms for general perception is of course common to Greek poetry as to human expression. The recurrence of such pleonasms as those cited cannot, however, be explained

away as chance or mere product of metrical convenience; they are too emphatic and too much directional.

19. E.g. the terms of linear order and arrangement in 167, 178, 298, 318, 387, 403, 516, 644, 660, 675, 730. Creon's military images also, as we have observed, stress a desire for an elemental and direct ordering of things that is then shown to be unable to comprehend or control the elements of personality which move Haimon and Antigone.

20. Cf. Werner Jaeger, "Praise of Law; The Origin of Legal Philosophy and the Greeks," in *Interpretations of Modern Legal Philosophies*, ed. by Paul Sayre (New York, 1947), pp. 352-75, for the historical development of the idea of law in Greek thought and for eloquent presentation of the conviction that "our Western tradition rests on this classical Greek construction of the world of law as presupposing a cosmos in which the human individual is related to a divine order of things." A more specific treatment of the philosophical conflict of *nomos* and *physis* in the fifth century is in Glenn R. Morrow's "Plato and the Law of Nature," in *Essays in Political Theory*, ed. by Knovitz and Murphy (Ithaca, 1948), pp. 17-44.

21. Cf. Jaeger, *ibid*, p. 361, " 'Civic virtue' was, in fact, the problem of problems for the ancient Athenians of the classical period, and the definition which is usually given of this concept is 'to be educated in the spirit of the laws.' "

22. E.g. 484-5, 525, 578, 678, 746.

23. 733-49: The argument includes the line οὐ τοῦ κρατοῦντος ἡ πόλις νομίζεται; (738): "Is not the city considered to belong to the ruler?", but also by the verb *nomizomai*: "Does not the city get its *nomoi* from the man in power?" Observe also the recurrence of the male over female relation as urged by Creon (746) and his charge in terms of practical legalism (742) versus Haimon, with the latter set off by Haimon's invocation of the justice and honors of the gods (743-5, 749).

24. Antigone's emphasis on kinship starts in line 1 and recurs again and again, e.g. 38, 45-6, 71-4, 503, 891ff., and includes stress on relationship in flesh and blood: *homosplagchnous* (born of same loins and womb) and *homaimos* (of shared blood) in 511-13.

Aristotle, in *Rhetoric*, 1, xiii, 2, uses Antigone to illustrate the notion of natural (*physei*) law. See also Erich Fromm's interpretation of "The Oedipus Complex and the Oedipus Myth," in *The Family: Its Function and Destiny*, ed. by R. Anshen (New York, 1949), p. 344.

25. As, for example, conflict between son and father which is manifested as such a prominent and brutal reality in the *Oedipus at Colonus* and generation of conflict between daughter and mother, partly through

and along the lines of similarity of personality, in the *Electra*. Cf. Fromm, *ibid*, pp. 334-58 on the former and Kitto, *op.cit.*, 132-4, on the latter.

26. The terms are there explicitly: *physis* in verbal form (905), *nomos* in 908 and 914, with the will of the citizens (907) and the metaphor of growth (911) implicit extensions of each side.

27. 1066: *tôn sôn . . . ek splagchnôn*, a strong and concrete expression, "one from your own very inwards," and one which echoes Antigone's term for her brothers, *homosplagchnous* (511).

28. Schmid in *Philologus*, 62, pp. 1-34, has marshaled most of the evidence by which Creon may be recognized as an ironic criticism of the Sophistic rationality and ethical relativism then coming into prominence. A similar conclusion is drawn by Egger, *Antigone-Problem*, pp. 67ff. It is pressed to extreme in W. Nestle's "Sophokles und die Sophistic," *Classical Philology*, 5 (1910), pp. 136-43. Cf. also Untersteiner, *Sofocle*, 2, p. 45 n. 21.

29. In Plato's retrospective accounts, most notably with Callicles in the *Gorgias* and Thrasymachus in the *Republic*, we find certain arguments that generally parallel but carry to emphatic direct statement the separation of *nomos* and *physis* (except in the right of the stronger) which is foreshadowed in Creon's use of these concepts. Schmid, *ibid*, p. 12, goes so far as to suggest that Sophocles' incorporation of the Sophistic *Geist* in the play is material for placing the first workings of Protagoras and Prodicus in Athens. But the state of our evidence being what it is we must be content with the more cautious kind of statement by which Jaeger, *loc.cit.*, p. 362, points to the obvious parallelism between the account of the origin of civilization in the second ode of the *Antigone* and the myth told by Protagoras in Plato's dialogue of that name: i.e. "it is hard to think there is no connecting link between the two."

30. Cf. Benjamin Farrington's *Greek Science: Thales to Aristotle* (Penguin Books, 1944), pp. 13-88, for a vivid account by an ardent naturalist of the rise of Greek science and its consequences in men's thought prior to the "Socratic revolution."

31. E.g. Democritus (fl. 420 B.C.), fr. 9: "Sweet exists by convention, color by convention; atoms and void alone exist in reality"; and Antiphon the Sophist (fl. latter half fifth century B.C.), fr. 44: "The edicts of the laws (*nomoi*) are imposed artificially, but those of nature (*physis*) are compulsory. And the edicts of the laws are arrived at by consent, not by natural growth, whereas the things of nature are not a matter of consent. . . . The majority of just acts according to the law are prescribed contrary to nature . . ." etc. H. Diels, *Die Fragmente der Vorsokratiker* (5th ed., Berlin, 1935), 2, pp. 139 and 346-8.

32. For detail and systematic treatment see Morrow, *loc.cit.*

33. *Loc.cit.*, p. 357.

34. *The Poetic Image* (Oxford University Press, Inc., 1947), p. 88.

35. The concept of complementary analogies at work in the elements of a play is developed fully by Francis Fergusson in *The Idea of a Theater* (Princeton, 1949); see especially pp. 35-41 and 234-6.

## APPENDIX

1. Robert Fitzgerald, in *Greek Plays in Modern Translation* (Dial Press, 1947), ed. by Dudley Fitts, p. 581.

2. So Gilbert Murray as reported by J. W. Mackail in *Lectures on Greek Poetry* (London, 1926) p. 145; also Stanford, *Aeschylus*, pp. 13-14.

3. *On the Sublime*, xxxiii.

4. *Op.cit.*, i, pp. 1-107, "The Language of Sophocles."

5. Obviously all studies of Sophocles' poetry cannot be quite so simply dichotomized. Kranz's treatment of the choral odes in *Stasimon*, pp. 174-227, is an excellent bridging of the analytical and appreciative, which centers on essential features rather than looking for idiosyncrasies, or vague excellences, though Kranz is somewhat preoccupied with a view of historically developing generic conventions and his book is colored by a concept of form as envelop for content.

6. These warning signs for the province of metaphor have been posted, respectively, by Allen Tate, *Hudson Review*, 1, p. 360; Stanford, *Metaphor*, p. 100; J. Middleton Murray, *Countries of the Mind* (Oxford, 1939), second series, p. 1. S. J. Brown's *The World of Imagery* (London, 1927) offers an extended theoretical analysis of figurative imagery supported by many examples from ancient as well as English literature and, with Stanford's book, is a useful guide into classical theories and practices.

7. Both ancient and modern theory support such an inclusive grouping. In Aristotle's four forms of metaphor (*Poetics*, xxi, 4; *Rhetoric*, iii, x, 7) the first two are strictly synecdoches and the third is a metonymy or hypallage, a transfer from *eidos* to *eidos*. For dissent with such compound grouping see E. M. Cope, *An Introduction to Aristotle's Rhetoric* (London, 1867), app. "On Metaphor," pp. 374-9; but cf. M. Murray, *op.cit.*, p. 3, and Brown, *op.cit.*, p. 26.

8. Cf. C. F. E. Spurgeon, *Shakespeare's Imagery* (New York, 1936), p. 9, and H. W. Wells, *Poetic Imagery* (New York, 1924), p. 23.

9. For a systematic discussion of the interaction of concrete and gen-

eral in metaphor, see the excellent section in T. M. Greene's *The Arts and The Art of Criticism* (Princeton, 1940), pp. 109-13.

10. The figure of overlapping circles to describe metaphorical imagery has been applied by many, including Brown, *op.cit.*, pp. 152-3, Wells, *op.cit.*, 21-2, Stanford, *Metaphor*, p. 105, D. A. Stauffer, *The Nature of Poetry* (New York, 1946), pp. 67-73.

I. A. Richards, in *The Philosophy of Rhetoric* (New York, 1936), pp. 89-112, established for what is now fairly common use the convenient tabs, *vehicle* and *tenor*, to distinguish the two ideas which any figurative image at its simplest gives us. The terms metaphor and image in their full sense should denote the composite or total effect produced by the interaction of vehicle and tenor. It should perhaps be emphasized, however, that the distinction between tenor and vehicle is more of a critical device for dealing with images than it is a necessary or accurate description of how the poet's mind works. A fusion of tenor and vehicle in a single, and often sustained, act of thought appears, in fact, to be a marked feature of Sophoclean diction. This fact is illustrated in particular in the following section of this Postscript (pp. 110-3), and recognition of it is fundamental to the understanding of the image patterns of the play. For a most discriminating treatment of this question of the interrelationship of tenor and vehicle—including its larger forms, the relations of theme and image, dialectic and rhetoric—see Rosemond Tuve's *Elizabethan and Metaphysical Imagery* (Chicago, 1947), and particularly chap. XII as of close bearing for the study of Sophoclean diction.

11. In the example given, it is fairly obvious that the connotations of "gilded" or of excessive magnificence and arrogance, which are sometimes evoked with the term *chryseos* and its related forms, do not apply here. The argument is not that the identification between vehicle and tenor must be complete but that it is likely to be a rich relationship and one which may operate on more than a single level. In this particular example (699) the notion of "brightness" is probably one of the strongest connotations for most readers because of the background of darkness in the preceding lines, 690-2.

12. *Op.cit.*, pp. 98-9.

13. 88: probably also, "Warm is your heart for those now cold (in death)."

14. An elaborate compilation and count of these types is to be found in W. Pecz's, "Vergleichenden Tropik der Poesie," Beitrag, *Berliner Studien fur klassische Philologie und Archaeologie* (Berlin, 1886), 3, pp. 1-172. He reckons the proportion of synecdoches and metonymies as against metaphors and similes in the three Attic tragedians as Aeschylus 1:6, Sophocles 1:3, Euripides 1:2.

15. Similes in dialogue: 424, 474, 477, 531, 712, 715, 1033, 1084; in odes, 110 and 586; in semi-lyric passages, 823, 826.

16. 823-33: Translation by Fitts and Fitzgerald, which in this case catches the total effect of the lines extremely well except for missing the sexual connotation in the last line.—Dudley Fitts and R. Fitzgerald, *The Antigone of Sophocles: An English Version* (New York, 1939).

17. 110-16: The last two lines of this anapestic system contain the translation of the eagle simile. The many shields of 115 are the white of the wing (cf. 106); the horsehair crests of 116 are obviously the plumage.

18. Cf. the personifications 295-301, 672-6, 1033-9, and a few others.

19. Cf. Wells, *op.cit.*, pp. 76ff. I have somewhat expanded the coverage of his term "sunken image."

20. 125-7: The presence of the "dragon" or snake can be felt in the phrase *amphi nôt(a)* (about its back, though also: behind him) and in the forceful coupling of the tensile verb, *etathê*, with a subject which is sound. The Scholiast's first note on the lines favors this concrete interpretation. Concrete connotations in the final phrase reinforce this sense of muscular strife: *antipalos*, a wrestling term; *dyscheirôma* a difficult "work of the hands," as well as "a hard victory" or "thing hard to overcome" by its more proper derivation from *cheiroô*. (Cf. Aeschylus, *Seven*, 1022, for *cheirôma* as though from *cheir*, hand.) In this interpretation it is immaterial whether datives or genitives are read in the last phrase. The genitive (of agent) is no doubt simpler, but the first reading of the ancient manuscripts is the dative (of agent or instrument).

21. Jebb in his commentaries on *Antigone*, 117, *Oedipus Tyrannus*, 866, and *Philoctetes*, 666, remarked particularly on what he calls Sophocles' tendency to "blur" images. "The image" (i.e. the vehicle), he says, "is slightly crossed and blurred by the interposing notion of the thing. . . . With Aeschylus, on the other hand, the obscurity of the image seldom arises from indistinctness of outline but more often from the opposite cause—the vividly objective (i.e. concrete) conception of abstract notions." This is true but, I think, misleading. In our terms Aeschylus is prone to extensive delineation of the vehicle which sometimes, at first glance, seems even to carry him away from the appropriate tenor; Sophocles, on the other hand, often blends tenor and vehicle closely and often does not pause to delineate his vehicle in detail.

Unfortunately Jebb gives no attention to what positive functions are gained by Sophocles' practice in this respect. As a term it is well, I think, to avoid "blurring" since it elevates a visual criterion and implies faulty photographic technique.

22. Cf. Campbell, note *ad loc.*

23. Wells, *op.cit.*, pp. 85, 92-9; Pecz, *loc.cit.*, pp. 162-5. In *Words and Poetry* (New York, 1928), pp. 237-8, G. H. W. Rylands seeks to show that as Shakespeare advanced, his use of metaphor became more subtle and more prone to such sunken forms as the coupling of an abstract with a vivid word of bodily action.

24. Stauffer, *op.cit.*, pp. 69 and 72, speaks to the point concisely: "Metaphor, then, in its wider senses, succeeds because it avoids the attempt to cover a subject by complete and direct statement. . . . The best comparisons are the subtlest . . . ," and again, "If a comparison can be more convincing than a flat statement, then, indeed, an implied metaphor may be more subtly powerful than a direct metaphor. . . . The reader of poetry, if he analyzes the reasons for the intensity of any poem, will find it often lies in comparisons that are never directly stated."

25. "Generalization is necessary for the advancement of knowledge, but particularity is indispensable to the creatures of the imagination," Rylands, *op.cit.*, pp. 56-7; cf. Stauffer, *op.cit.*, pp. 120-53; Wells, *op.cit.*, p. 94, "The capacity of the metaphorical imagination is to generalize upon the concrete, and the particular is at the basis of poetic imagery." For a telling confirmation by a poet in respect to just such Sophoclean images as we have been considering see Shelley's observations on the *Oedipus Tyrannus*, 67. "In the Greek Shakespeare, Sophocles, we find the image *pollas d'hodous elthonta phrontidos planois* a line of almost unfathomable depth of poetry; yet how simple are the images in which it is arranged! 'Coming to many ways in the wanderings of careful thought!' " Shelley goes on to urge that the words do not simply represent something vaguely general like "ways and means" or "wanderings" in the sense of error and confusion but that they represent "literally paths or roads, such as we tread with our feet; and wanderings such as a man makes when he loses himself in a desert, or roams from city to city—as Oedipus, the speaker of this verse was destined to wander, blind and asking charity. What a picture does this little line suggest of the mind as a wilderness of intricate paths, wide as the universe which is here made its symbol. . . ." (Quoted in "Note on *Prometheus Unbound* by Mrs. Shelley," in *The Complete Works of Percy Bysshe Shelley* [Oxford, 1935], p. 269.)

26. Cf. A. L. Keith's *Simile and Metaphor in Greek Poetry* (Menasha, Wis., 1914), a very thorough and perceptive catalogue of images by subject, author by author, from Homer through Aeschylus. Many parallel citations from earlier poets are included in F. M. H. Blaydes' useful collation, *Spicilegium Sophocleum* (Halle, 1903), pp. 37-139.

27. E.g. Stanford, *Aeschylus*, pp. 86-7 and Headlam in *Classical Review*, 16, p. 442.

28. E.g. *Biographia litteraria*, xv, 3.

29. Cf. Hoppe, *De comparationum et metaphorarum apud tragicos Graecos usu* (Berlin, 1859), pp. 4-5, and G. Radtke, *De tropis apud tragicos Graecos* (Berlin and Krotoschin, 1865 and 1867), part i, pp. 24-5.

30. Cf. Stanford, *Metaphor*, pp. 142-3 for the relation of Homer and Aeschylus to the probable state of a poetic diction at their respective times. For a general discussion of the existence and function of an established poetic diction (or dictions) in the Greco-Roman world see G. Murray, *The Classical Tradition of Poetry* (Cambridge, 1927), pp. 122-46.

31. 399: *kai krine kàkselegch(e)*; cf. Aeschylus, *Eumenides*, 433. In 60 and 632 there seems to be a certain underlying irony in the use of the term *psêphos* (properly: pebble, but especially a voting ballot) for Creon's edict, which as the action progresses becomes less and less a matter of popular choice and more and more his single "vote"; cf. Aeschylus, *Suppliants*, 373, for an obvious use of this term to compress the opposition between single leadership and popular voting. Cf. also 159-60 for two technical terms of the Assembly; possible legalism in *ophliskanô* (469-70), (*ap*)*agousi* and *kathelontes* (381-3); and a possible formula of oath in 266.

32. See particularly *Frogs*, 795-802 and 1364-1413, where measuring rods, foot-rules and scales for calculating the bulk and weight of poetry are put to fine comic use. Cf. on this J. W. H. Atkins, *Literary Criticism in Antiquity* (Cambridge, 1934), I, p. 27.

33. Not only the work of Pecz and Earp's elaborate tables, which have already been described, but also Schmid, *Geschichte . . . Literatur*, 2, pp. 465-6, and T. B. L. Webster, *An Introduction to Sophocles* (Oxford, 1939), pp. 152-3. For compilations by subject matter there are Radtke, *op.cit.*, images from agriculture, sailing, and hunting; Hoppe, *op.cit.*, birds only; D. Bassi, "Il sentimento della natura in Sofocle," *Rivista de filologia*, 12 (1884), pp. 57-103, and P. Rödström, *De imaginibus Sophocleis a rerum natura sumptis* (Stockholm, 1883), various types of images from nature; E. Kritchauff, *Questiones de imaginum et translationum apud Sophocleum usu* (Lyck, 1882), sea and weather only; G. Lueck, *De comparationum et translationum usu Sophocleo* (Neumark, 1878 and 1880, Stargardt, 1882), 3 parts, covering agriculture, public institutions, and war; Louis Morel, *De vocabulis partium corporis in lingua Graeca metaphorice dictis* (Geneva, 1875), bodily images.

34. E.g. Lueck, *op.cit.*, part 3, pp. 5-6, 10-11.

# BIBLIOGRAPHY

‧◝◝◝◝◝◝◝◝◝◝◝◝◝◝◝◝◝‧

NOTE: This list is designed simply to list in five general categories the various books and articles which I consider particularly pertinent to the several aspects of this study. If it serves as a guide to others its purpose will have been fully met. It should at the least illustrate in itself some of the range and some of the intricacies of the study of imagery and structure in dramatic poetry.

## I. CRITICAL THEORY

### A. CLASSICAL

ATKINS, J. W. H. *Literary Criticism in Antiquity* (Cambridge, 1934), 2 vols.: vol. 1, chaps. 1, 2, 3, 4, 6, and vol. 2, chaps. 1, 2, 6.

BUTLER, H. E. *Quintillian, Institutio oratoria* (Loeb Lib., New York, 1922): esp. bk. VIII, vi.

BYWATER, I. *Aristotle on the Art of Poetry* (Oxford, 1909): text, commentary, translation.

COPE, E. M. *An Introduction to Aristotle's Rhetoric* (London, 1867): esp. appendix "On Metaphor," pp. 374-9.

FRÄNKEL, E. "Aeschylus: New Texts and Old Problems," *Proceedings of The British Academy*, 28 (1942), pp. 237-58: esp. pp. 249ff. on critical method.

HEADLAM, W. "Metaphor, with a Note on Transference of Epithets," *Classical Review*, 16 (1902), pp. 434-42.

KEITH, A. L. *Simile and Metaphor in Greek Poetry* (Menasha, Wis., 1914).

MURRAY, G. *The Classical Tradition in Poetry* (Harvard Univ. Press, 1927): chap. 4 on meter, chap. 5 on poetic diction.

ROBERTS, W. RHYS *Longinus on the Sublime* (Cambridge, 1899): text, translation, introduction, and stylistic appendix.
*Dionysius of Halicarnassus: The Three Literary Letters* (Cambridge, 1901): similar to above.
*Demetrius on Style* (Cambridge, 1902): similar to above.
*Dionysius of Halicarnassus on Literary Composition* (London, 1910): similar to above.

SANDYS, J. E. *The Rhetoric of Aristotle* (Cambridge, 1877), 3 vols.: esp. bk. III, chaps. 2-5, 10-11.

SPENGEL, L. *Rhetores Graeci* (Leipzig, 1884-94), 3 vols.

# BIBLIOGRAPHY

Stanford, W. B. *Greek Metaphor* (Oxford, 1936).
*Ambiguity in Greek Literature* (Oxford, 1939).
*Aeschylus in His Style* (Dublin, 1942).
Tate, Allen "Longinus," *Hudson Review*, 1 (1948), pp. 344-61.

## B. MODERN

Brooks, Cleanth *The Well Wrought Urn* (New York, 1947): esp. pp. 3-20, 176-238.
Brown, S. J. *The World of Imagery* (London, 1927).
Downer, Alan S. "The Life of Our Design," *Hudson Review*, 2 (1949), pp. 242-63.
Empson, Wm. *Seven Types of Ambiguity* (London, 1930).
Fergusson, Francis *The Idea of a Theater* (Princeton, 1949).
Greene, T. M. *The Arts and the Art of Criticism* (Princeton, 1940): esp. pp. 3-25, "Introduction," and 98-119, "The Matter of Literature."
Lewis, C. Day *The Poetic Image* (Oxford, 1947).
Macbeth, J. W. V. *The Might and Mirth of Literature* (London, 1876).
Müller, Max *Lectures on the Science of Language*, 2nd series (London, 1886), lecture VIII, "Metaphor."
Murray, J. M. *Countries of the Mind*, 2nd series (Oxford, 1939), ch. 1, "Metaphor," pp. 1-16.
Prior, Moody E. *The Language of Tragedy* (New York, 1947): esp. introductory analysis, pp. 1-16.
Ransome, J. C. *The New Criticism* (Norfolk, 1941).
"Poetry: I, The Formal Analysis," *Kenyon Review*, 9 (1947), pp. 436-56.
Richards, I. A. *The Philosophy of Rhetoric* (New York, 1936): esp. chaps. 5 and 6 on metaphor and chap. 3, "The Interinanimation of Words."
"The Interactions of Words" in *The Language of Poetry*, ed. Allen Tate (Princeton, 1942).
Rylands, G. H. W. *Words and Poetry* (New York, 1928).
Spurgeon, C. F. E. *Shakespeare's Imagery* (New York, 1936).
Stauffer, Donald A. *The Nature of Poetry* (New York, 1946).
"Genesis or the Poet as Maker," in *Poets at Work*, ed. Abbott (New York, 1948), pp. 37-82.
Stevens, Wallace "The Noble Rider and the Sound of Words," in *The Language of Poetry*, ed. Tate (Princeton, 1942), pp. 91-125.
Tuve, Rosemond *Elizabethan and Metaphysical Imagery* (Chicago, 1947): esp. chap. 1 and part 2.

URBAN, W. M. *Language and Reality* (New York, 1939): esp. chap. 3, "Language as the Bearer of Meaning," and chap. 10, "The Language of Poetry and Its Symbolic Form."

WELLS, H. W. *Poetic Imagery* (Columbia University Press, 1924).

WHEELWRIGHT, PHILIP "Poetry, Myth, and Reality" in *The Language of Poetry*, ed. Tate (Princeton, 1942).

WINTERS, YVOR *Primitivism and Decadence* (New York, 1937).

## II. STYLISTIC STUDIES

(see also within III below)

BRUHN, E. Anhang, vol. 8, of Schneidewin-Nauck *Sophokles* (Berlin, 1899): a grammatical and stylistic appendix.

CAMPBELL, LEWIS *Sophocles* (Oxford, 1879), 2nd ed., 2 vols.: text, commentary, and introductory essay, "On the Language of Sophocles," vol. 1, pp. 1-107.

EARP, F. R. *The Style of Sophocles* (Cambridge, 1944).

HABERLANDT, O. *De figurae quae vocatur etymologica usu Sophocleo* (Freienwalde, 1897).

HEMMERLING, J. *Sophocles quo iure Homeri imitator dicatur* (Cologne, 1868/9).

HOPPE *De comparationum et metaphorarum apud tragicos Graecos usu* (Berlin, 1859).

JACOBI, F. *De usu alliterationis apud Sophoclem* (Goettingen, 1872).

KRICHAUFF, E. *Quaestiones de imaginum et translationum apud Sophoclem usu* (Lyck, 1882).

KUEHLBRANDT, H. *Quomodo Sophocles res inanimas vita humana induerit* (Leipzig, 1880).

KUGLER, L. G. E. *De Sophoclis quae vocantur abusionibus* (Goettingen, 1905).

LECHNER, MAX *De rhetoricae usu Sophocleo* (Hof, 1871).

LOB, J. *Die Verwendung des homerischen Wortschatzes bei Sophokles* (Salzburg, 1909).

LUECK, G. *De comparationum et translationum usu Sophocleo*, parts 1 and 2 (Neumark, 1878 and 1880), part 3 (Stargardt, 1882).

MACKAIL, J. W. *Lectures on Greek Poetry* (London, 1926), pp. 139-77, on Sophocles.

NAVARRE, OCTAVE *Essai sur la rhétorique greque avant Aristote* (Paris, 1900): esp. pp. 102-11 on Sophocles.

PECZ, W. "Vergleichenden Tropik der Poesie," Beitrag, *Berliner Studien für klassische Philologie und Archaeologie* (Berlin, 1886), vol. 3, pp. 1-172.

"Die Tropen der Ilias und Odyssey," *Neue Jahrbücher für das klassische Altertum*, 29 (1912), pp. 664-70.

RADTKE, G. *De tropis apud tragicos Graecos*, part 1 (Berlin, 1865), part 2 (Krotoschin, 1867).

RÖDSTRÖM, P. *De imaginibus Sophocleis a rerum natura sumptis* (Stockholm, 1883).

SCHAMBACH, C. *Sophocles qua ratione vocabulorum significationes mutet et variet* (Nordhausen, 1878).

SCHIRLITZ, KARL *Das Bildliche in den Tragoedien des Sophokles* (Wernigerode, 1870): very general.

STEVENS, P. T. "Colloquial Expressions in Aeschylus and Sophocles," *Classical Quarterly*, 39 (1945), pp. 95-105.

THOMAS, ROBERT *Zur historischen Entwickelung der Metapher im Griechischen* (Erlangen, 1891): lexicographical.

## III. GREEK TRAGEDY AND SOPHOCLES: GENERAL STUDIES

BLUMENTHAL, ALBRECHT VON "Sophokles (Aus Athens)," Paulys *Real-Encyclopaedie der classischen Altertumswissenschaft* (Stuttgart, 1927), 2nd series, vol. 5, cols. 1040-1094.

*Sophokles* (Stuttgart, 1936): esp. pp. 104-6, diction, and 145-63, *Antigone*.

BOWRA, C. M. *Sophoclean Tragedy* (Oxford, 1944).

DE FALCO, V. *La tecnica corale di Sofocle* (Naples, 1928), pp. 36ff. and 204ff. on *Antigone* and general principles.

FITTS, D. *Greek Plays in Modern Translation* (New York, 1947): incl. notes pp. 541-96.

HAIGH, A. E. *The Tragic Drama of the Greeks* (Oxford, 1896): esp. pp. 126-203, 348-88.

HENSE, O. *Der Chor des Sophokles* (Berlin, 1877).

HYDE, W. W. "Sophocles' Place in Greek Tragedy," in *Classical Studies in Honor of John C. Rolfe* (Penna. Univ. Press, 1931), pp. 115-41.

JAEGER, WERNER *Paideia* (New York, 1945): vol. 1, esp. pp. 268-85.

JEBB, R. C. *Sophocles, The Plays and Fragments* (Cambridge, 1892-1907), 7 vols., including the *Antigone* (3d ed., 1900) as vol. 3: text, commentary, introductions, and translations.

*Essays and Addresses* (Cambridge, 1907): pp. 1-40, "The Genius of Sophocles."

KITTO, H. D. F. *Greek Tragedy, A Literary Study* (London, 1939): esp. chaps. 5, 6, 7, 10.

KRANZ, WALTHER *Stasimon* (Berlin, 1933): esp. pp. 175-227, "Das Chorlied der klassischen Tragoedie."

# BIBLIOGRAPHY

Lucas, F. L. *Tragedy: In Relation to Aristotle's Poetics* (New York, 1928).

Moore, J. A. *Sophocles and Aretê* (Harvard University Press, 1938).

Muff, C. F. *Die chorische Tecknik des Sophokles* (Halle, 1877).

Müller, Adolf *Aesthetischer Kommentar zu den Tragoedien des Sophokles* (Paderborn, 1913): esp. pp. 34-52, 93-122, 439-96.

Nauck, A. *Sophokles*, ed. F. W. Schneidewin and A. Nauck (Berlin, 1868-1899), 8 vols. including *Antigone* (9th ed. 1886) as vol. 4: critical text, commentary, introduction, textual appendix.

Nestle, W. "Sophokles und die Sophistik," *Classical Philology*, 5 (1910), pp. 129-57.

Norwood, G. *Greek Tragedy* (London, 1920).

Patin, Alois *Aesthetisch-kritische Studien zu Sophokles* (Paderborn, 1911) in *Studien zur Geschichte und Kultur des Altertums*, vol. 4, part 4.

Pearson, A. C. *Sophoclis fabulae* (Oxford, 1923): critical text.

Pohlenz, Max *Die griechische Tragoedie* (Leipzig, 1930): esp. pp. 158-63, 186-202, 226-39.

Post, C. R. "The Dramatic Art of Sophocles," *Harvard Studies in Classical Philology*, 23 (1912), pp. 71-128.

Rahm, A. L. S. *Über den Zusammenhang zwischen Chorliedern und Handlung in den erhaltenen Dramen des Sophokles (und Euripides)* (Erlangen, 1907): esp. pp. 68-87 on Stasima I, II, and IV of *Antigone*.

Reinhardt, Karl *Sophokles* (Frankfurt, 1933): pp. 75-105 on the *Antigone*.

Robert, Carl *Oidipus* (Berlin, 1915), 2 vols.: vol. 1, pp. 332-80 and vol. 2, pp. 119-29 on *Antigone*.

Saunders, A. N. W. "Plot and Character in Sophocles," *Greece and Rome*, 4 (1934), pp. 13-23.

Schmid, W. Schmid-Stählin *Geschichte der griechischen Literatur*, vol. 2 (Munich, 1934): pp. 309-513, Sophocles, esp. pp. 486-500 on his diction.

Schroeder, Otto *Sophoclis cantica* (Leipzig, 1907): metrical study.

Sheppard, J. T. *Aeschylus and Sophocles, Their Work and Influence* (New York, 1927), pp. 40-81: generalized description.

*The Wisdom of Sophocles* (London, 1947): appreciative essay.

Shorey, Paul "Sophocles," in *Martin Classical Lectures, I* (Harvard University Press, 1931), pp. 57-95.

Thirlwall, C. "The Irony of Sophocles" in *Remains, Literary and Theological, of Connop Thirlwall*, ed. J. J. S. Perowne (London, 1878), 3 vols.: vol. 3, pp. 1-58.

UNTERSTEINER, MARIO *Sofocle, studio critico* (Florence, 1935), 2 vols.
WEBSTER, T. B. L. *An Introduction to Sophocles* (Oxford, 1936): esp. chap. 7, "Style," and chap. 6, "Song."
WEINSTOCK, HEINRICH *Sophokles* (Leipzig, 1931), pp. 97-126, "Staat/ Antigone."
WILAMOWITZ MOELLENDORF, TYCHO VON *Die dramatische Technik des Sophokles* (Berlin, 1917): pp. 1-50 on *Antigone*.

## IV. ANTIGONE: PARTICULAR STUDIES

(see also III above)

AGARD, W. R. "Note on *Antigone*, 904-20," *Classical Philology*, 32 (1937), pp. 263-5.
BAYFIELD, M. A. *The Antigone of Sophocles* (London, 1901): text and commentary.
BRACKETT, H. D. "An Alleged Blemish in The Antigone of Sophocles," *Classical Journal*, 12 (1916-17), pp. 522-34.
BUTTMANN, A. *Abhandlung über das zweite Stasimon in des Sophocles Antigone* (Prenzlau, 1869).
COWSER, J. "The Shaping of the *Antigone*," *Classical Association Proceedings*, 36 (1939), pp. 38-40.
DEWITT, NORMAN W. "Character and Plot in The Antigone," *Classical Journal*, 12 (1916-17), pp. 393-6.
DRACHMANN, A. B. "Zur Composition der Sophokleischen Antigone," *Hermes*, 43 (1908), pp. 67-76.
EGGER, P. J. B. *Das Antigone-Problem* (Solothurn, 1906).
ERRANDONEA, I. "Sophoclei chori persona tragica," *Mnemosyne*, 50 (1922), pp. 369-422, 51 (1923), pp. 180-201, 297-326, 52 (1924), pp. 27-60.
"Über Sophokles Antigone, 944-987," *Philologische Wochenschrift* (1930), cols. 1373-5.
FITTS, D. and FITZGERALD, R. *The Antigone of Sophocles: An English Version* (New York, 1939).
FLICKENGER, M. K. *The Hamartia of Sophocles' Antigone*, in *Iowa Studies in Classical Philology*, 2 (1935).
FRIEDLÄNDER, P. "Πολλὰ Τὰ Δεινά," *Hermes*, 69 (1934), pp. 54-63.
HEWITT, J. W. "An Unobserved Bit of Sophoclean Irony," *Classical Philology*, 25 (1930), pp. 383-6.
HORRMANN *Die Construction der Antigone des Sophokles* (Detmold, 1858).
HUMPHREYS, M. W. *The Antigone of Sophocles* (New York, 1891): text and commentary.

JOHNS, W. H. "Dramatic Effect in Sophocles' *Antigone*, 1232," *Classical Journal*, 43 (1947), pp. 99-101.

KAIBEL, G. *De Sophoclis Antigona* (Goettingen, 1897).

KNAPP, CHARLES "A Point in Interpretation of *Antigone* of Sophocles," *American Journal of Philology*, 37 (1916), pp. 300-16.

KOCKS, D. W. *Die Idee des Tragischen, enwickelt an der Antigone des Sophokles* (Cologne, 1858).

MEAUTIS, G. "La psychologie de l'*Antigone* de Sophocle," *Rivista de filologia*, 66 (1940), pp. 25-27.

MURRAY, G. *Sophocles, The Antigone* (New York, 1941): verse translation with notes.

PETERKIN, L. D. "The Creon of Sophocles," *Classical Philology*, 24 (1929), pp. 263-273.

SCHLESINGER, EITHARD "Δεινότης," *Philologus*, 91 (1936-7), pp. 59-66.

SCHMID, W. "Probleme aus der Sophokleischen Antigone," *Philologus*, 62 (1903), pp. 1-34.

VALLE, E. DELLA *Saggio sulla poesia dell' Antigone* (Bari, 1935): concerned with drama rather than poetic language.

VLACHOS, N. P. *The Subject of Sophocles' Antigone* (diss., Univ. of Pennsylvania, 1901).

VOLLGRAFF "Ad Sophoclis Antigonam," *Mnemosyne*, 46 (1918), pp. 71-82, 174-83, 358-67, and 48 (1922), pp. 366-8: esp. 48, pp. 374-9 on personified Dikē.

WYCHERLEY, R. E. "Note on Sophocles' *Antigone*, 904-20," *Classical Philology*, 42 (1947), pp. 51-2.

## V. MISCELLANEOUS

BASSI, DOM. "Il sentimento della natura in Sofocle," *Rivista de filologia*, 12 (1884), pp. 57-103.

BLAYDES, F. H. M. *Spicilegium Sophocleum* (Halle, 1903): esp. pp. 37-139.

BOWRA, C. M. "Sophocles on His Own Development," *American Journal of Philology*, 61 (1940), pp. 385-401.

BOYNTON, M. F. *Tragic Hamartia in the Iliad, the Odyssey and Sophocles' Antigone* (typewritten MA Thesis, Cornell University, 1935).

BURKE, KENNETH "The Imagery of Killing," *Hudson Review*, 1 (1948), pp. 151-67.

BUTCHER, S. H. *Aristotle's Theory of Poetry and Fine Art* (London, 1898), 2d ed.: esp. chap. 8, "The Ideal Tragic Hero," and chap. 9, "Plot and Character in Tragedy."

COOPER, LANE *Aristotelian Papers* (Cornell University Press, 1939), pp. 131-52, "The Villain as 'Hero.'"

COPLEY, F. O. "The Pathetic Fallacy in Early Greek Poetry," *American Journal of Philology*, 18 (1937), pp. 194-209.

ELLENDT, F. *Lexicon Sophocleum* (Berlin, 1872).

ELLINGHAM, C. J. "Classical and Modern," *Greece and Rome*, 6 (1937), pp. 144-55.

FROMM, ERICH "The Oedipus Complex and the Oedipus Myth," in *The Family: Its Function and Destiny*, ed. R. Anshen (New York, 1949).

HEADLAM, W. "Ghost-Raising, Magic and the Underworld," *Classical Review*, 16 (1902), pp. 52-61.

JAEGER, W. "Praise of Law: The Origin of Legal Philosophy and the Greeks," in *Interpretations of Modern Legal Philosophies*, ed. Paul Sayre (New York, 1947), pp. 352-75.

JEBB, R. C. The "Introduction" in *The Attic Orators* (London, 1876), 2 vols.: esp. vol. I, pp. xcii-ci on Greek tragedy and Sophocles.

KOBER, A. E. *The Use of Color Terms in the Greek Poets* (Geneva, N.Y., 1932).

"Some Remarks on Color in Greek Poetry," *Classical Weekly*, 37 (1934), pp. 189-91.

LEES, J. T. "The Metaphor in Aeschylus" in *Studies in Honor of Basil L. Gildersleeve* (Baltimore, 1902), pp. 483-96.

MORROW, G. R. "Plato and the Law of Nature," in *Essays in Political Theory*, ed. Knovitz and Murphy (Ithaca, 1948), pp. 17-44.

O'CONNOR, M. B. *Religion in the Plays of Sophocles* (diss. Chicago, 1923).

PAPAGEORGIUS, P. N. *Scholia in Sophoclis tragoedias vetera* (Leipzig, 1888).

PEARSON, A. C. *The Fragments of Sophocles* (Cambridge, 1917), 3 vols.

SCHMIDT, J. H. H. *Synonymik der griechischen Sprache* (Leipzig, 1876-86), 4 vols.

SOUTAR, G. *Nature in Greek Poetry* (Oxford, 1939).

STAMBLER, BERNARD *The "Villain" in Greek Drama* (typewritten MA Thesis, Cornell University, 1932): esp. pp. 68ff.

TARRANT, D. "Imagery in Plato's *Republic*," *Classical Quarterly*, 40 (1946), pp. 27-34: esp. on image-groups and reiterative imagery.

# INDEX OF REFERENCES
## TO THE TEXT

~~~~~~~~~~~~~~~~~~~~~~~~~~~~~~~~~~~~~~~~

169

# INDEX